PURSUED BY PURPOSE

Uplifting Stories Of Courage Under Pressure

———

A Compilation by Debra Wright

RMK PUBLISHING

Toronto, Canada

Pursued By Purpose: Uplifting Stories of Courage Under Pressure
Copyright© 2021 by Debra Wright All rights Reserved. This book or any portion of this book may not be reproduced or used in any manner whatsoever without the express written permission of the publisher except for the use of brief quotations in a book review.

Printed in Canada First Printing, 2021

RMK Publishing

DEDICATION

*This book is dedicated to you, the reader
who has come through many challenges in life
and has gained a greater understanding of
your purpose in life.*

Debra M. Wright

Contents

	Pursued By Purpose Copyright© 2021 by Debra Wright. *Uplifting Stories Of Courage Under Pressure* Debra Wright	xi
	Introduction *Uplifting Stories Of Courage Under Pressure* Debra Wright	1
	Foreword *Uplifting Stories Of Courage Under Pressure* Patricia Bebia Mawa	5
	ACKNOWLEDGEMENT *Uplifting Stories Of Courage Under Pressure* Debra Wright	7
1.	GREAT VIEW FROM THE REAR-VIEW MIRROR Carla P Caprietta	9
2.	DO AS I SAY NOT AS I DO Christie-Ann Nicholas	19
3.	LIFE AFTER DEATH Dr. Maria Caprietta	29
4.	WHO YOU SAY I AM WILL NEVER DEFINE ME Pauline Danquah	41

5.	THE ROAD TO BECOMING A CITIZEN	53
	Cindy Forbes	
6.	JOURNEY FROM WITHIN	63
	Rose M Young	
7.	PURPOSE FUELED THROUGH PAIN	73
	Marlene Mae Henry	
8.	THE PURSUIT OF PURPOSE	81
	Glen Prince	
9.	LETTING GO	93
	Anna Pereira	
10.	THE LOVERMORE MASTERPIECE	103
	Lovemore Sher McLaughlin	
11.	A PATH TO VICTORY	115
	Nicole Waldron	
12.	COMING TO CANADA	127
	Blessing Ajayi	
13.	JOY COMES IN THE MORNING	141
	Debra Wright	
14.	I'M A BIG GIRL NOW	151
	Cheryl Moses	
15.	AGAINST ALL ODDS	161
	Carlton H Wright	
16.	NO DRAMA	171
	Ruth Dente	
17.	LEARNING TO WALK AGAIN	183
	Christie-Ann Nicholas	

18.	BEHIND CLOSED DOORS Vanya Caprietta	193
19.	LIFE'S LESSONS Debra Wright	203

Part I. A QUEEN

Part II. I Feel Your Pain!!

CONCLUSION	219
Notes	225
Publishers Note *Uplifting Stories Of Courage Under Pressure*	227
Other Books by Author	229

Pursued By Purpose Copyright© 2021 by Debra Wright.

Uplifting Stories Of Courage Under Pressure

Debra Wright

Cover design by D. Wright

Stonehouse Media

Cover photo: Canva

All rights reserved. This book or any portion thereof may not be reproduced or used in any manner whatsoever without the publisher's express written permission except for the use of brief quotations in a book review.

Printed in Canada First Publishing 2021

Published by: RMK Publishing Toronto Canada

Introduction

Uplifting Stories Of Courage Under Pressure

Debra Wright

This anthology is a collaboration of seventeen powerful and different persons who have endured some incredibly challenging circumstances throughout their lifetime but were able to arrive at the same conclusion.

They were Pursued by Purpose!

Our stories are no different from anyone of you that have had challenges that may have seemed insurmountable, yet you found your purpose because of or despite.

I am thrilled to have found these amazing men and women with whom I could share my vision so that we can bring these stories of healing to life. The stories that they have shared are from their personal experiences, their struggles, their pain, and their triumphs.

In life, nothing goes linearly, or should I say a straight line. There are many curves, hills, and sometimes many rivers to cross to pursue our happiness or just this thing called life.

For those of you reading this book, your life may have been wrought with many twists and turns, and you are wondering, what is happening to me? Why can't I figure out where I am going?

I know, I have been there and, I know that there will be one or more if not all the stories that resonate with you. However, these stories will let you know that there is light at the end of the tunnel and that you will arrive at your destination stronger than ever.

I want to share with you the definition of Pursued and Purpose. (Websters Dictionary)
Pursued: To be followed by someone or something to attack
Or to follow to overtake, capture, kill, or defeat.
to find or employ measures to obtain or accomplish
seek to pursue a goal.

Purpose: The reason for which something exists or is done.
An intended or desired end, goal, determined resolution.

As I look at the purpose, the scripture Jeremiah 29:11 comes to mind, and it contains a precious promise held dear by Christians the world over. ... In this verse, Jeremiah affirms that God is in control. He has good things in store: *"For I know the plans I have for you, declares the LORD, plans for welfare and not for evil, to give you a future and a hope."*

When the purpose pursues, you never really make excuses because you are not looking for something. Things happen to and for you.
When you face the challenges that life throws at you, you don't have a choice, keep putting one foot in front of

the other, and eventually, you will realize that you have come to a place that you did not know you were heading.

Purpose can also be described as a lifelong journey, as was previously stated, with many twists and turns arriving at your destination.

We may think and believe that to find your purpose, and you need to do a course or go to university; honestly, many people find their life's purpose by stumbling upon it, by the events that transpire in their lives.

I believe that what we experience in life will help us reflect on who we are and what problem we can help to solve in the world.

I like to think about what God thinks about being pursued by purpose, and Psalm 139:7-8 ESV says.

"Where shall I go from your Spirit? Or where shall I flee from your presence? If I ascend to heaven, you are there! If I make my bed in Sheol, you are there!"

If I understand this scripture, it says that his spirit is with us always, and we can't really flee from his presence, so it is safe to say that he pursues us by always being there beholding what we are going through?

Where you are today is not by happenstance, it is because of your journey, the people in your life that either supported or devastated us, or probably our own interests and experiences. My prayer is that you will see yourself in this book and begin to identify with it and hopefully gain some insight that you are not alone and that God is using your setback as a setup for greatness. Your test will become your testimony, your mess your message, and you will be able to share and help others.

For you, our readers, please get a nice hot cup of cocoa, tea, coffee, or a nice cold drink, curl up and enjoy the gifts and nuggets found in this book. Mark the pages and see yourself in them as we have struggled and made it through becoming better versions of ourselves, so to can you.

Stay blessed and encouraged.

Debra M Wright

Foreword

Uplifting Stories Of Courage Under Pressure

Patricia Bebia Mawa

Finding your purpose is about self-discovery, and this may take some time. The good news is that you do not need to look too far. It just requires intentionality and inquisitiveness. The best thing that can happen to a person is to find their "Ikigai." This is a Japanese word which, interpreted, means "a reason to live," or our life's purpose.

Pursued By Purpose is an anthology that features the stories of seventeen remarkable men and women who have faced their fair share of challenges but are still standing strong and living a purpose-fuelled life. The profundity of their stories reveals their struggles, pain, and victories. These men and women have given us a gift as they share their experiences to learn from the past, enlarge our perspectives and transform our lives.

Everyone has a story, but not everyone shares their story. Sharing your story does not just help you free yourself, but it is a sign of growth and progress. It shows that you have moved beyond your experiences and learned some lessons. Stories are a common denominator of human existence.

As you read this book, you will have moments of trepidation, awakening, amazement, and celebration. Some of the stories will resonate with you and validate your own experiences. They will make you realize that you are not alone in whatever you are going through. Someone somewhere somehow is experiencing the same thing or worse. I Peter 5:7 says," *We should cast all our cares on Him for He cares for us.* The underlying factor in these stories is that these men and women believe in the unmovable power of God and are pursued by purpose.

As we navigate the journey of life, we learn from the roads we have traveled to guide our steps to the future. Maturity is learning to walk in your own shoes. Your steps may not be steady, but you learn to get up each time you fall with long practice. The strength to go through the storm is in you! Unfortunately, we sometimes look for help elsewhere not to drown while wearing the life jacket.

> *"When you are born, make room for a name.*
> *When you are called a name, make room for yourself*
> *When you are yourself, you impact the world*
> *When you impact the world, people will then know you*
> *When you are known, do not forget your name*
> *If you forget your name, you will be out-of-place."*

Like the seventeen incredible men and women featured in this book, be pursued by purpose. Decide to focus on opportunities, not obstacles, destination and not roadblocks, and your potential and not your shortcomings. As each day passes, you are painting the portrait of your life. Use faith as your canvas, purpose as your brush, and prosperity as the promise of your brilliance.

Patricia Bebia Mawa
Television Executive, Publisher, Author & Thought Leader

ACKNOWLEDGEMENT

Uplifting Stories Of Courage Under Pressure

Debra Wright

I want to thank my husband, Carlton, for always being my number one supporter, friend, and confidant. Whenever I bring you another project, you never discourage me but always encourage me to soar.
Thanks, my love. Love you forever!

I want to thank my mother and father for the many hours of prayers and always being willing to listen to me when I have struggled through life and needed a shoulder to cry on. You're an inspiration not just to me but to many others as well.

To my most amazing children Christie-Ann, Joe, and Christopher, for the joy they have brought to my life and for giving me those adorable grandchildren Roman, Milan, and Kaliah, and more...

My bonus blessings to Bethany, Jen, and Maurice; thank you for sharing your dad with me.

I want to thank my amazing coauthors for deciding to join me on this journey. I know that this process for some of you has stretched you and has allowed you to accomplish your goal of becoming a published author. Our lives will be forever intertwined.

Thank you, Rose Young, for being a friend and the person that introduced me to the world of anthologies and as my former compiler in the Bestseller Broken Trust Anthology.

Last but certainly not least, I want to thank my heavenly father for always being there for me even when I stumble and sometimes fall. Your word says that" *Weeping may endure for a night, but Joy comes in the morning."Psalms 30:5*

1.

GREAT VIEW FROM THE REAR-VIEW MIRROR

Carla P Caprietta

As I sit to pen my words, staring into my laptop computer screen, I am reminded of that time that I sat at a computer for the very first time, some 20 + years ago. The personal computer was a new invention at that time and without the *"worldwide web,"* I might add! There was a limit to what that computer could do then, but it was the beginning of a massive technological change in hindsight. Today, the personal computer has been revolutionized, and there are still many more milestones to be reached with this technology.

Just like the computer, my life has also been revolutionized over the years. What seemed to be an amazing beginning for me in my early adult life, a beautiful blue sky with a silver lining over the horizon, came to a crashing halt. *But God!*

Marriage was a distant thought for me in my teenage years. In my heart and mind, I had my future planned out very well. I wanted to do all the Science courses, excel in school, become a Medical Doctor, travel the world for a little while, then get married, maybe in my early 30s. We plan our lives, but sometimes we leave ourselves open for the enemy to wreak havoc with our plans.

After graduating from High School, my family and I migrated to Canada for greater opportunities. We were that family who loved God so much that my family would be one of the two, if only two families were at a church meeting. God meant everything to my parents, and he certainly meant everything to me. Soon after we were settled in Canada, we found a church that catered to our belief system. It was at this church that my now ex-husband locked his gaze on me. Medical School was not as pressing now as it was in the past because the hurdles to get into the program were challenging and quite different to my home country, the beautiful Island of Trinidad. However, the offer of marriage then looked very attractive, and I surrendered to the call.

When I got married at the tender age of 21, it felt like I achieved the goal I didn't know I needed. I felt like it was the beginning of a beautiful life with endless possibilities, my *"Forever After."* As the years rolled on, my desire to become a Medical Doctor diminished, but it never left my heart. From time to time, I would be asked medical questions by my family, friends, coworkers, and other random characters. Yes, God finds ways to show you his plans for your life even when you stray. For example, he designed me to be a "healer" when I was a child because whenever I saw anyone injured or feeling ill, it would hurt me deeply, and I would wonder how I could heal them.

My marital bliss started dwindling after a few short years. I started feeling the wind of turmoil. We both worked, but the bills piled up, the credit card bills got bigger, words got harsher towards me when we were alone, but the picture to those that were on the outside looked blissful. As a woman, I started picking up little ques that all was not as it seemed. God opened my eyes to the possibility of infidelity. I searched all over and eventually found that letter that you were never supposed ever to see. It was the unveiling of the reason for my uneasy feelings, otherwise known as intuition. Explanations, flowers, and beautiful words could not take that uneasy feeling away from me. Nothing made sense. We were Christians, together we were serving God, so there should not be any problems such as this, or so I thought.

There were a few years of calm, however other problems arose, and I got more and more buried under fear and grief. My family meant the world to me, and they were always a part of my life, but my dysfunctional marriage caused an unforeseeable rift in me that I really was not prepared for. I had questions about whether my family was truly the problem, which I was always made to feel. Time spent with the family was getting shorter and shorter. The quality times we spent together were gripped with anxiety on my part. There would be lingering fearful thoughts that these precious gatherings, visits, or trips might come to a painful halt one day. The family never left me to slip away unnoticed. At times I felt their questions, which I never allowed them to speak. They truly were there when I needed them without them knowing that I did need them that much.

The questions that I had about my family were unfounded. I truly had no reason to feel unease with my parents nor my siblings. What I mean by that is, I grew up with these people, we had wonderful times together, and the way we showed love to each other was as if it was Christmastime every time we got together. But the subtle hints that were thrown out to me were not who I thought they were plagued my mind for years. My parents were truly very caring, not only for their family but for so many others that it truly was impossible to think otherwise.

My parents still blessed my home with their punctuation of visits ever so often. My parents were very much in my life, and I trusted their opinions. Because of their upbringing in my most impressionable years, I became the beautiful person I am today. They cared for and guided my siblings and me to serve God with fervency and be kind to others. I am so grateful that my family never left me to "drown." They were there for me at the close of my marriage. I was such a strong but silent person that they truly did not know the extent of what I encountered, but they all rallied around me and nursed me back to "life."

In growing up, I was the strong silent type, and I was not easily swayed. I was settled in who I was and where I wanted to be in life. I held strong to my dreams, and I kept myself from the temptations of youthfulness. However, as I grew, I became more fearful of things, speaking up, of people in authority, and voicing my opinions. I internalized my fears. I was a young lady of few words, but the love and care I had for people went truly deep. People found it very easy to talk to me because I was a great listener, and my words were few and far between. When I spoke, it was taken as great wisdom. Marrying at the age of 21 to someone with a strong personality and strong views about things overshadowed my ambitions, and it pushed me deeper into my internal space. I developed a Dependent personality. The plans that I had for my life were now overshadowed by the mundane and the plans of someone else's.

In the last few years of marriage, I got so much closer to God. I started desiring the baptism of the Holy Ghost. I heard this topic preached quite a few times before, but it was that one time, preached by my brother-in-law-to-be (at that time), that it pricked my heart, and I sought the Lord fervently. Then God gave me some beautiful experiences until that day that he filled me with his Holy Spirit. My soul came alive. Things looked good at home for a little while, but then it took a turn for the worst. I sought the Lord, and he heard my cry, time and time again. Then it happened! I was no longer relevant to my husband.

When the hand of God brought me out of a failed marriage, he first gave me peace. That very morning after, that beginning of my "single-ship," I awoke with a peace that I never knew before. No fights were going on in my head, no voices, no fear, nor any questions, just a peace that I call the "Peace that passes all understanding."

The God that we serve is caring, loving, and true to his word. So God says, in Jeremiah 29:11 KJV, *"For I know the thoughts that I think toward you, saith the Lord, thoughts of peace, and not of evil, to give you an expected end."*

Within two (2) weeks of my separation, I heard a song playing in my head as I lolled off to sleep one night. I heard as if there was a throng of people singing and playing instruments, including tambourines, dancing in the streets. I heard the chorus and the verse, of which I eventually awoke, grabbed a pen and paper in the dark, and wrote.

As I lolled off to sleep again, I heard other verses, and I quickly wrote them down as well. It was a beautiful song to Jesus, saying that I will wait and run this race, I will wait in victory because our Lord is coming back. What an amazing way to start a new journey, a new chapter of my life. God started me on my way, he gave me peace, and he gave me a song in the night, and This was the beginning of my songwriting portfolio.

As the weeks rolled on, something was changing in me without me realizing it. I was talking. At first, it was talking about my past and what I suffered in silence in my marriage. I regurgitated the past several times in that season until I no longer felt the need nor desire to talk about it. What that exercise did was amazing. Firstly, it helped me purge; secondly, it helped me release my inhibition of speaking about my life. The third thing that came out of the exercise was that it got me talking. From this point, my family realized that I was involved in conversations, and on numerous occasions, I was the one talking the most. This change in me was a revolution. Now there was no stopping to what God could do.

One month after my separation, my ex-husband asked me what I would do next. The words rolled off my tongue so quickly and beautifully, as I said, "I am going to become a doctor." Those words came from a deep place because I did not speak those words before that day until I was confronted. As I spoke those words, the plan of God started to unfold. *Sometimes, we have to speak it out for that thought or desire to be manifested.* Immediately after, I gathered information from the various Universities, enrolled in school, and now hold a (Hon) Bachelor of Science degree in Biological Science.

I am grateful to God that I went to university as a mature student. You see, at this stage of my life, I was no longer a quiet, shy, or fearful person; it was quite the opposite. I joined school clubs, and I was the Vice President of the Caribbean African Students Association (CASA), Orientation Leader, Mentor, and Science Fair assistant. I was a friend to many, and my best friends called me "miss popular." I even found myself getting the portfolio of "editor," as many of my friends asked me to edit their assignments. This change in me is the height of what God can do with a vessel that is yielded to him. You see, my life had been a life of serving Jesus. I sought the Lord when I was in trouble, and he heard my cry and delivered me.

My path to Medicine did not happen the way I planned it. God allowed me to go through my mess; after *all, it was my choice,* but he gave me a reset. He now gave me friends who subscribe to some of the same principles, passions, and desires as I do – to serve God with all our heart, love people, and the love for the field of Medicine.

Did you know that God could position you into things and places that you never thought you would ever be able to get to? Yes, he does. I went to Med School on a beautiful Dutch Caribbean Island. I went to this school with one of my best friends. We made many new friends, but we were inseparable. Not too long after being on the Island, we found a bible-believing church. We visited and realized that we were delighted with their singing and their teachings. It was in our second semester that the Pastor's mom approached me right after church one Sunday. She heard me singing and confronted me, saying, **"you sing**?" I was shocked at the question. She proceeded to tell me that she heard me singing as she pulled me along to introduce me to the Worship Pastor. That meeting not only gave me an adopted grandmother, who she became, but I also gained two of my best friends, a Pastor and a Prophetess (power-couple).

Before long, I was one of the worship leaders at church. This appointment right here is a victory! Previously, I was timid, fearful, introverted, and afraid of singing in public. Whenever I was asked to sing a solo at church, I refused. However, when I did accept, the fear that came over me was so thick that I would close my eyes and sing. Whilst walking away from the podium, I trembled all the way back to my seat with fear. *But here I am leading worship, and there's no trepidation? "Wow!"*

I was given the President of the Student Christian Medical Dental Association position at school by one of my best friends, the club president. He sought the Lord and felt the leading to make me his successor. I refused until it was evident that it was indeed what God wanted me to do. I was also the choir director of the group. I assisted in organizing a concert for the youth of our church. Our choir did a wonderful job that night. As a group, we also assisted at an after-school children's program, organized bake sales, and had weekly group prayer with sharing the Word of God. *You see, at this point, I did not recognize myself, but I loved the new me. God radically changed my life.*

Getting back home after such great experiences, I was now onto another level of victory. God opened the door for a leadership role at a church. I became the Worship Pastor under the leadership of an amazing and anointed Pastor.

I am a witness that there is no stopping to what God will do when you yield yourself to and put your trust in him. If God can do this for me, then what God cannot do does not exist!

Carla P Caprietta is a Health and Wellness Coach, a worship minister, and a Teacher of the Gospel. She has a passion for seeing people healed from sickness, diseases, and mental strongholds holistically. She was a Mentor, a Vice President of the Caribbean African Student Association, President of the Christian Medical Dental

Association, and Music Director of the CMDA choir at university.

Carla's first degree was in Biological Science, and she is currently pursuing her degree in Naturopathic Medicine. She says, "I love seeing people healthy, and I believe that the Natural Holistic approach is the way God intended it to be."

Contact: starcapvoice@gmail.com

https://www.facebook.com/carla.caprietta2

Instagram: @carlacaprietta @capricarla

@healthycopia

2.

DO AS I SAY NOT AS I DO

Christie-Ann Nicholas

Our parents are most often our first teachers in this life. They are our first love. They clothe us, provide shelter and food, as well as love and care for us. They are our protectors and our guide. But whether it is intentional or not, our parents also hurt and disappoint us. I learned many lessons from my parents by simply observing them. I spent many years processing the hurts brought on by my parents until I was finally old enough to understand and forgive them.

I had an awesome childhood growing up. I lived in a two-parent home along with my two younger brothers. Both of my parents were involved in my upbringing. My dad was the one who taught me how to tie my shoes and ride a bicycle, as well as rollerblading. My mom taught me how to bake and do laundry and how to do my hair, even if I was not all that great at it. We took family vacations together, went to church together, and went on many countryside drives, all as a family. Being young, I never saw just how distant my parents really were. I was happy to be with both my parents. I had friends in school who told me about their parents living separately and going from one house to another, their parents constantly fighting and yelling in front of their children. I was so grateful that was not me.

At the age of 12, my parents had bought their first home. In my mind, this was going to be ours forever. At first, I was not happy with the location because I was so far away from all my friends, but it quickly grew on me when I saw the size of my room. I was not concerned with sharing; being the only girl had its perks, but being the oldest also gave me the biggest room, after my parents. It was in this house that I began to see the distance between my parents.

I never saw any real affection between my mom and dad, but I did not question it because I never heard them yelling or fighting with each other. I figured that must be what love was. My grandparents on my father's side were never married, but they lived together all their lives, albeit in separate rooms. They rarely showed affection to each other as well. I had only traveled to Trinidad a couple of times to spend summer break with them, and watching them interact with each other was rather distant, but at such a young age, I just believed that was how they loved each other. My grandparents on my mother's side, although sometimes reserved, showed more affection towards each other, but I knew that they loved each other. I could not explain as a child, but as an adult, I knew it was genuine. All the couples around me were quite reserved in showing affection to each other but were very liberal in showing affection. I did not question it because I knew my family loved me; my family wanted me.

As I came into my teenage years, I grew distant from my dad. We barely spoke two words to each other, and it frustrated me. I could not understand how a father could stop talking to his daughter, his only daughter. I had seen so many stories about how a father is supposed to be his daughter's first love, and I did not have that. But I also watched my parents a little harder and realized they were not as in love as I thought they were. There was no real affection between them, no communication of any sort. So finally, at 16 years old, I told my mom, "Maybe you should get a divorce. I would be okay with that because you guys aren't even happy." When I said it out loud to my mom, I realized just how sad it made me. All this time, I was priding myself on the fact that I was not a statistic. I was still in a two-parent household as a teenager, whereas many of my friends grew up with stepparents. But saying it aloud made it real; what I was encouraging my mother to do would make me a statistic, and being a person of color just made it even worse because black families were mostly made up of single mothers and their children with no father in sight.

As I grew older and dreamed about marriage, I began to picture a marriage like my grandparents on my mother's side. I admired their relationship. They would have their little quarrels but made up quickly. My grandpa had love in his eyes for my grandma and her for him. I longed for the day when someone would look at me the way grandpa looked at grandma. But I was looking for that love in all the wrong places. I could not relate to my dad. I could barely even talk to him about my day, let alone relationships. I could talk to my dad about anything in my childhood, but my teenage years into adulthood without my father were tough and confusing. He was physically present but withdrawn, and that to be equated to an absent father.

In 2013 my mom told me that they were separating,

and it was heading to divorce. It brought me back to my 16-year-old self of not wanting to be a statistic but knowing I would be okay with their decision. It felt like someone had died. My family called to tell me they were sorry, and I did not want to hear it. I knew for years that my parents were not happy together. I told myself I would never have a marriage like theirs, and I made it my mission to do better than them; to be like my grandma and grandpa. But I was still devastated. My family was coming to an end, and I did not have anyone to comfort me.

I spent the next few years angry with my dad and in and out of terrible relationships. Then, I met my future husband, in 2015 and I was finally starting to feel happy. He made me feel appreciated and had patience with me. I talked to him about all the issues I had since my parents' divorce, and he listened to me. I told my mom about my then-boyfriend, and eventually my dad as well. Neither had yet to meet him as my mom lived in Trinidad, and my dad was in a city about two hours away. I did not see much of my parents, but I was happy because I had my boyfriend.

In 2016, my boyfriend joined the US military, and I was alone. It was depressing. Luckily, he had met both my parents. My mom had returned from Trinidad for an event, and I introduced her to a man who would later become her husband. Unfortunately, my dad got married later that year, and I was angry. How could he marry someone that I was not even introduced to? He invited me to the wedding, and I declined. Looking back now, I regret it, but I was just too angry at the time. And watching my mom fall in love was not easy.

While my boyfriend was away, my family and I traveled

to minister and sang at different events. Although I was 25, my attitude was that of a teenager, and I could not understand it. Mom had told me about her relationship while she was in Trinidad, and I was genuinely happy for her even though, at first, I was upset with her boyfriend. I could not understand why he would make a move on my mother. Seeing my mother being affectionate in front of me, in front of our family, irritated me. I hated every moment of it so much so that I would isolate myself.

I had to process my feelings because I knew I was making it difficult for my mom, but I could not help my reaction. I had never seen my mom be affectionate with another man; I had never even heard pet names uttered from her lips unless it was to her children. My mom and I ended up arguing. She told me she did not understand why I was acting the way I was and that I should be happy for her. She told me how confused and hurt she was by my actions, and I told her I did not understand it. I told her that she could not tell me how to feel. The truth was this situation was new for both of us. She was navigating life as a newly divorced woman, and I was watching her do so with someone other than my father. It would be another year and a half before I came to terms with my new life and that of my parents.

When I was younger and thought about getting married; and my dad was who I pictured when I was walking down the aisle. In the years after my parents split, I did not really care if my dad was there or not. The whole situation emotionally damaged me. I told my mom that I would not mind if my brother walked me down the aisle. I had the opportunity to sit down with my dad for lunch one day, and for the first time in a long time, we had a conversation.

Even though my boyfriend and I were still dating, I knew that we would get married. He told me, so himself and I took great comfort in that. I told my dad that we were thinking about marriage and hesitated before telling him I was unsure if I would want his new wife there. It would be my wedding, and I should have a say in who attends and who does not. I could tell that it hurt my dad, but I had to say it because, deep down, it was the truth, and I was still upset about what had transpired between us while I was growing up. My dad did not say much after that. He respected what I had to say, and for that, I was grateful because he acknowledged my feelings.

In 2017 I got married. There was a lot of chaos going on, and I was afraid that someone would stop me from getting married. There were so many tears and emotions on the day of the wedding. My dad walked me down the aisle, and I will forever cherish that moment. My husband and I lived at my grandparents' house for the first few months of our marriage, and I was so grateful to be with them because they were my example of marriage. Even with me being married, I was still having trouble accepting my mom's new relationship, and soon they would be marrying. The months leading up to my mom's wedding were a disaster for me. I could not accept her public displays of affection. On the day of the wedding, however, I was able to push past my feelings and support her.

But the words "stepmom" and "stepdad" started to pop up everywhere in other people's vocabulary when talking to me, and it irritated me to my very core. It did not matter if they were married to my parents; I could not call them to *step* anything because they did not parent me. By the time my parents had separated, I was already an adult. It made me feel like even more of a statistic. So I was not too fond of it. I attended church with people who had assumed my mom's husband was my father and called him as such. I would smile and tell them he is not my father. Inside I was screaming, but I never let it show because they did not know.

As I began to navigate marriage in my own life, I realized I had adopted many bad habits from my parents and saw things just like my parent's marriage, which scared me. For the first few months, staying with my grandparents gave us a foundation as we saw my grandma caring for my grandpa as his health declined while still maintaining a home and keeping it filled with love. I always wanted to communicate with my husband, and I did my best to ensure that we did. Still, after many years of watching my father, I had developed the habit of being quiet when unhappy and completely shutting down. Something that I am still working on to this very day.

When my husband and I finally moved into our own place, my relationship with both my parents was being mended. I watched them in their own marriages and then watched my own and knew that things would be different for all of us.

In 2019 I met my dad's wife for the first time, and I was so proud of myself for the simple fact that I smiled and introduced myself. I was not even angry. I did not have any resentment or unforgiveness. Time had run its course, and I was okay with that. Daddy and I continued to mend our relationship. Although I may not be friends with my dad's wife, I know that we will be able to sit and have a conversation with each other at some point and maybe build a relationship from there. Likewise, my relationship with my mom's husband has pretty much been restored to what it was before he met my mom.

I have realized that some things heal and restore only with time. I needed to be honest with myself and my feelings about my parents' divorce. Even though they are no longer together, and I am now a statistic, as sad as it sounds, I am happy because my parents are happy. Because of my parents' example of marriage, I realized what I did and did not want for myself and my husband. And when my children come, I can show a healthier example of what it means to love. I could have used my parents' divorce and my relationship with my father as an excuse to stay broken and wallow in sorrow. I could have used my parents' relationship as an excuse every time something went wrong in my marriage. I am sure that my parents did love each other when they got married, but sometimes it does not work out, no matter how hard you try. But thanks to them, I intend to do things differently with my family. I will break the generational curses for my family.

Life is all about choices. When it comes to relationships, what type of partner will you be? When it comes to children, what type of parent? There are many examples all around us, and we can either choose to turn a negative into a positive or continue down the negative path. We understand that parenting looks different for everyone, and if you are blessed with children, make sure to take the time and apologize to them; they are people who will grow and build their own families.

Christie-Ann is a singer, writer, and actress. At the young age of seven, Christie-Ann developed a passion for creative arts. Inspiring her to become a vocalist, featured on several albums, and was
involved in various productions. In addition, Christie-Ann wrote many poems and short stories.

Christie-Ann enrolled in Toronto Film School, graduating with honors, where she wrote and directed a short film dedicated to her sister and went on to host a television show, "Open Mic."
Christie-Ann is currently working on her first podcast series and hopes to create books and television shows for families and direct short films.

Contact: cgnoreiga@gmail.com

28 Debra Wright

https://www.facebook.com/cagnicholas

https://www.instagram.com/chrissiegrace_/

3.
LIFE AFTER DEATH
Dr. Maria Caprietta

It is not common to get married in society today, and it is even less common to stay married. As a result, there are very few couples whose marriages have stood the test of time, overcome trials, and survived, even in death. Grieving the loss of one's long-time spouse can be a journey, as you now must rediscover who you are as an individual while seeing reminders of them in your everyday life.

I believe in my heart that my life began when I met the man of my dreams, my husband. We had spoken briefly before at church, but once my father took notice, he advised Percy to ask permission to "speak to his daughter." My father then told him that he needed to "limit his visits" until I had finished my college exams, as education came first. So, after my college graduation, Percy and I began courting with my father's permission, and things progressed quickly. Then, suddenly, Percy stopped coming to visit, and it remained that way for a few weeks before he returned. He would later tell me that he became scared because he did not want his relationship to end up like his parents, who had a broken marriage.

Percy and I grew remarkably close, and soon there were

talks about marriage. My parents invited him to come over, and the four of us had a long talk, which felt like an interrogation. It was a serious discussion, but thankfully God worked it out. At the end of it all, I accepted the proposal of marriage.

Wedding plans quickly came together. It was a short engagement, and on June 19th, 1966, Percy and I got married. We were excited about our new life together. On our wedding night, Percy spoke these words to me, "Maria, we will not break this marriage. It will last until death. I will not walk in the footsteps of my dad and mom, who had a broken marriage." We agreed and prayed concerning what he had just spoken about. I was moved to tears by Percy's words, but I also cried because I missed my family.

During our honeymoon, we met an older gentleman who imparted a few words of wisdom which stayed with us throughout our marriage. He said, "never go to bed angry with each other, make things right, pray, then go to bed."

When we returned from our honeymoon, we went back to my parents' home to live, and life resumed. I was an active member of my father's church, and I was the president of the Youth Association. Part of my responsibilities was putting concerts together, directing productions, writing plays, and directing the choir. In addition, I organized many outings and cookouts. Percy was an ordained minister who would travel to various churches, and as his wife, I would go with him. When we were not traveling, I was teaching Food Preparation and Nutrition in the community.

Two months after we were married, my mom passed away from complications during childbirth, leaving behind eleven children ages one day old to twenty-one. It was a terrible time for me as a new wife and a mother figure to my younger siblings. In the beginning, it was exceedingly difficult for Percy; however, he was soon able to adjust to this new reality, stating that he "would be there for everyone."

During the first year after my mother's passing, I became a new mother, and some of my siblings were separated as there were too many of us. Some went to live with my grandmother, others went to my aunts, and some stayed with me. My dad migrated to Canada, remarried, and shortly after, sent for his children.

When my father left, his church closed, and my husband and I started attending another church. I was not as active in the church since I became a new mother and had another child on the way. However, I did join the prayer group and continued to work part-time as a teacher.

As the years passed and more children came, I was grateful that I could continue working teaching in the community. Having the support of my husband encouraged me to go further with my career. I decided to switch career paths and worked as a Cook, a Home Management Teacher, and a Food Service Supervisor in the Hospital.

One day, my husband and I talked and considered migrating to Canada for a better life. We were content with our life in Trinidad but wanted more for our family. So, a few months later, we moved to Canada and began a new life.

Coming to Canada allowed my husband to graduate from college and while he continued working as a barber. In Trinidad, he worked in the Defense Force and was the assigned barber to the President of Trinidad and Tobago for many years. I obtained my Canadian certifications and began working as a Food Service Supervisor at a Hospital. I worked in the hospital for six years before starting my own Party Rental and Catering business. I took courses in long-term care management, floral design, and travel and tourism at that time. I was always interested in higher education and pursued it while taking care of my family. My husband supported me through all my endeavors.

Five years after opening my business, I had to make the difficult decision to close it. Once the business was closed, I got the opportunity to work with my daughter and assisted her with event planning and wedding décor. With the closing of my business, my husband and I could travel more and care for our grandchildren. Our children were now grown, and some went on to get married. I transitioned from being just a parent to being a friend. *Life was good!*

Several years and many grandchildren later, I decided to go back to school. It was during this time that my husband was diagnosed with Parkinson's' Disease. Hearing this news was devastating, yet we were optimistic that God would bring us through. A few months later, my husband retired and stopped driving. It was difficult for me to process this.

I knew how much my husband enjoyed barbering and driving; driving in the countryside was a favorite pastime.

At the beginning of my husband's retirement, we took walks regularly, and while I furthered my education, my husband spent a lot of time with our sons, fishing. Our last momentous fishing adventure was when our son drove with us to South Carolina. My husband seemed to be like a teenager, experiencing the joys of catching fish. As a wife, I could not have been happier. I was remembering the many moments of watching him teach his children and grandchildren how to fish.

As my husband's condition worsened, I became a caregiver while still in school. It soon became overwhelming for me to take care of my husband by myself and attend in-person classes. I requested homecare which we arranged shortly thereafter. Between constant trips to the hospital and doctor's appointments for my husband, I successfully finish my classes.

The holiday season of 2017 was extremely difficult for me. My husband was admitted to the hospital, and there were conversations with the doctor that he may not survive the next few days. I had made the decision that I would not leave his side. I was praying that he would live to see me graduate with my doctorate. My husband recovered and was released a few weeks later.

My husband had a few more brief stays in the hospital over the next two years. During this time, I put all my energy and attention into taking care of him and neglected myself. A few weeks before my graduation, my husband was admitted to the hospital, and I again prayed that he would be there to see me graduate. He recovered and was sent home. The night before my graduation, my husband was again admitted to the hospital, and I was devastated.

I was in between attending my graduation and being with my husband. My children advised me that it would be good to attend, and someone would stay with him. Although he was not physically with me, he was alive and aware of this major event, and that was enough for me. When graduation was over, I quickly returned to my husband's side.

As a wife, you believe that your husband will be with you forever, but I could see in his eyes that he was becoming tired of the way life was. He told me, on separate occasions, that he was seeing angels. Finally, he yelled out, "there's a lot of them. They came to fellowship with us." I wanted so badly to see what he saw, and I could not, but I felt an awesome presence.

He and I spoke about our family starting a business, and he told me to pursue my goal. I told him that he needed to be with me, and he happily agreed, but it was not meant to be. A few days later, my husband would be admitted to the hospital and not return home. On the last day of my husband's life, the doctor informed me that he did not have long to live and gather the family to say their last goodbyes. All our children and their families came to visit. We sang songs and enjoyed our time together, and he transitioned the following morning.

After my husband passed, I felt lost, my best friend was gone, and I was alone. However, I was happy to know that he was not in pain anymore; there was no more suffering. He had transitioned to be with God, and I realized that I had to continue living with purpose.

My final goodbye to my husband of 53 years, although difficult, was a beautiful celebration of life. Seeing our seven children, their families, and my friends come together to celebrate this man I loved so dearly will be etched in my mind for as long as I live.

I was now adjusting to a life that did not include my husband. I was no longer his caregiver. I felt lost and as though I no longer had a purpose. I knew what my husband had told me to do, but I could not pursue it at that time. My mind was so hazy, and I was overcome with grief. I was rarely seen without my husband; he was my traveling partner. After his passing, I lost my desire to travel. Thanksgiving and Christmas were vastly different that year as it was my first year without him. Soon after my birthday, my children advised me that it would be best to get away for the winter, which I normally would do. I almost declined, but my sister agreed to travel with me.

During my trip, I cried a lot. Visiting family and friends who were very dear to us made me realize how lonely I was because we would always travel together. Unfortunately, he was not there to share in these new memories. Amid my grief, I am grateful that I decided to travel, and I enjoyed my trip.

A week after my return, the country shut down due to the pandemic. This was a difficult time for me as my grief was very much present. There was nothing I could do to distract myself from the pain I was feeling. Everything was closed, and I could not go outside or visit friends. There was not much to do anymore, but I was grateful that social media and phone calls could still connect me. Eventually, I was able to start processing my grief. I realized that you could not rush grief; it must take its course. There were days when I woke up and cried; other days, there was lots of laughter. My children became a pillar for me during this time but having my grandchildren around brought me so much joy to my heart.

Many families were separated because of the pandemic, but I was grateful my children and their families still came to visit. Seeing this scene before me reminded me of my dream to see all families reconnected. I have observed that families are no longer what they used to be. The media's portrayal of families today is one of division. There are many broken homes and marriages.

As a happily married woman for 53 years and birthed 7 children, I saw the importance of having both a mother and father in the home while rearing children. Having my family worshiping and praying was the foundation for raising our family. I am reminded of the words my father said to me, "the family that prays together stays together."

I have witnessed and experienced the effects of divorce and its implications on children and adults with people around me. Unfortunately, due to my husband's broken home and the trauma he experienced, he was afraid for us when he realized our relationship was heading towards marriage, but ours lasted. Seeing these heartbreaking situations before me has stirred up my desire also to help married couples. I want to help them see that they do not have to repeat the cycle and make a better choice than their parents. Because my husband decided to be better than his parents, our marriage lasted until death. We cherished each other, had respect for one another, and had open communication on all levels.

My mind and heart are also for the elderly. Sometimes we believe that when we reach a certain age, we stop growing. But there is still a lot more than you can do with your life. I received my Ph.D. at the age of seventy-four. I am still pursuing university courses, and I may go back for another degree.

In this season of grieving and lock-down, I realized that I still had so many things to accomplish. I was able to rediscover who I was, apart from my husband, not as a wife but as a person, as a woman. I am aware that this season would require God's grace and comfort to enable me to navigate through life; I cannot go it alone. There are so many memories, circumstances, family, and friends to remind me of my husband. This was truly one of the most difficult challenges that I have had to face in life. Losing a spouse is heartbreaking; however, I know that God is my comforter and my strength.

I am surrounded by love, families and friends, phone calls, and visits; the list goes on. They are there to remind me of my purpose amid my grief, and I am determined to achieve my goals just as I told my husband I would.

Dr. Maria Caprietta is a Clinical Counsellor, Psychotherapist, Dynamic Speaker, Life Coach, and Founder of The Family Hub.

Her life passion is to empower people for greatness. "I love people and have a passion for young people. They are the leaders, employees, and parents of tomorrow."

Her interest inspires Dr. Maria's work in Health and Wellness. She is an expert in Food, Marriage, and Family Counseling. In addition, she specializes in areas of Longevity in Marriage, Long-term Care, Healthy relationships, Conflict Resolution, and Child/Youth Development. Dr. Maria motivates people to excel in life and think outside of the box. She is the author of "Crossroads," a life-changing book.

Contact: mariacapri7@gmail.com

https://www.facebook.com/maria.caprietta

https://www.mariacaprietta.com/

4.

WHO YOU SAY I AM WILL NEVER DEFINE ME

Pauline Danquah

I will never forget hearing from my high school guidance counselor that I was disqualified from post-secondary education simply because I enrolled in applied courses. It made me feel stupid to be told I would not be admitted to university. Within the span of two minutes, I went from happy and expectant to feeling as if my life had been shattered. As a young adult, I felt my life had come to its lowest point of hopelessness, and I was devastated. My expectations when I walked into that office were high; I expected to pick courses for university like all my friends, little did I know that my dream of pursuing higher education would be replaced with the most devastating news for me. My stomach was in knots, and I felt ashamed of myself. What would I say to my parents? How was I going to tell my friends? The feeling of being left out was overwhelming. I was a high school student without a career path. Where was I supposed to go from here? All this time, I had trusted my school to help me succeed, but at that very moment in that office, I felt let down. I suddenly understood what it meant to be a student who has fallen through the cracks.

During this time, I had a lot of questions on my mind.

I felt like a reject and a failure after leaving that office. I could not understand how this could have happened because I had grades at least in the B range. My grades were average... My counselor made me feel like there was no other choice in that office, and I regret letting her assert that power over my feelings. I felt wronged, even though I knew there had to be another way.

My middle school grades made me insecure about my ability to take academic courses in high school, so I chose applied courses. Although I have always been a B student, certain courses in math, science, and English have always been my biggest struggles. Doubting my ability to succeed academically led me to choose applied courses in the first place, and although I had not failed in high school, I still found it shocking that I would be denied the opportunity to choose courses for university like my peers.

In the past, I remember my older sister feeling discriminated against by the same guidance counselor. As part of my sister's grade 12 academic requirements, she needed six academic courses to apply to science programs in university, but she was told she could not take physics with her other science and math courses because she would struggle to handle the load. Although this is good advice for weaker students, her counselor did not look at the grades and courses she had taken in grade 11 to see that, in fact, she was clearly strong enough academically to take all six courses in grade 12, rather than splitting them and coming back for one more year. I admire my older sister so much, as she was a straight-A student and is now pursuing a career in medicine to become a doctor. But she was judged based on the colour of her skin. The unfortunate thing about these situations is that they often occur to people of colour. In a way, this proves that my high school could have failed both myself and my older sister.

While graduating with my graduating class, and having received a letter from my principal for the Ontario Scholar (honour roll) award, I still was not satisfied that I could not attend university. The fact that I believed my counselor so much that I did not apply anywhere made me feel as if there was no way out. My biggest fear was that the university responses would be disappointing if I applied. So, I took two years off after high school to figure out what I wanted to do, and I eventually went to college.

While studying General Arts and Science and playing on the Sheridan women's soccer team, I was caught up in distractions and questioned whether I would succeed. I simply did not seem as motivated as I should be, and I was overwhelmed with doubts. After my second year of college, I quit school and went to work. My self-identity and self-worth were still not satisfactory to me. I was trying to figure out if I had overcome the pain of doubting my strengths; at that time, I was still unsure what kept me from becoming the woman I was meant to be. However, I finally completed college, graduated, and applied to university. I enrolled in the same year and began my journey to success.

Getting into university was one of the best things that ever happened to me. At 26, I wondered, am I too old? Five years ago, all my friends graduated from university! Despite being accepted to university, I felt a little embarrassed. However, the moment I arrived there my life changed completely for the better. Originally from Brampton, I attended Algoma University in Sault Sainte Marie, ON, Canada. As a dual major, I studied Law &

Justice and Political Science. Throughout my undergraduate career, I developed more self-confidence and began to dominate where I thought I could overcome my doubts of success.

The first year as a student at Algoma, I ran for the Vice-President of Campus Affairs executive position for the Algoma University Students' Union (AUSU). After securing a successful campaign and winning the election, I was so proud to have been able to make it this far! I had no idea what I was preparing myself for, but there was a small voice inside me telling me to push forward, that this is what I had to do. As such, I did it. In the following year, I ran for President and was elected. In my university's history, I was the first female Black president; that was a milestone, a challenge, and a breakthrough. No way did I ever think I would ever become president of an entire university! I shed tears of joy and excitement; the experience reminded me that I was supposed to be here in the first place, and that those same words I received from my guidance counselor did not define me.

I worked so hard during the campaign, and I met a lot of wonderful people from diverse backgrounds. I spent every single day, in person and online, listening to my peers and describing my values, beliefs, and the policies I wanted to change and implement for the student population. The whole election was the highlight of my twenties, and I can never forget the feelings I experienced or the person I became afterward. From that moment onward, I felt undefeated, as if I had been rejuvenated.

As a result, I broke through even more barriers. I started public speaking and advocating for social justice issues which led to appearances on local news, live interviews, and being featured on multiple Toronto billboards, magazines, and subway station ads in Brampton and Sault Ste. Marie. I am sorry, but how amazing is it to be on more than one billboard!? Such an opportunity does not come around often, but I was blessed with it by my university, this is another moment I will cherish forever. Additionally, I participated in protests and demonstrated my commitment to social justice issues in the streets of Sault Ste. Marie and Toronto.

Furthermore, I successfully ran for the Women's Constituency Commissioner in Ontario for the Canadian Federation of Students. It was a privilege to become the public voice for many women in Ontario, creating safer spaces for us to speak about gender issues and how they negatively impacted our education, cultures, jobs, and our everyday lives. I also ran for the position of Constituency Commissioner of Ontario for the same organization and won. I enjoyed this position because it gave me an opportunity to interact with students of different backgrounds and identities. I advocated for students on a wide range of topics including mental health, education, and our everyday lives.

Finally, while I served as president of AUSU, I implemented the very first black graduation ceremony. Some may have reacted negatively to this because they questioned why it was only for Black students. Or the other question, isn't it then reasonable to have separate graduations for all races? My view is, there is no harm in making your own for your race, but your WHY is what matters. Black graduation to me was significant because so many of us had come from so many different contexts and backgrounds to a predominantly white community.

In this small town, we formed our own little community, cultivated our own small victories, and celebrated our small successes even though we did not all come from Black Canadian backgrounds. Racism, microaggressions, and discrimination were also common occurrences.

In North America, graduation is also a big deal, and it is one of the most important days of our lives. But at a Black graduation ceremony, it is not a quiet ceremony! We chant, sing, and cry together as we receive this great accomplishment. But for some of us, our lives are shortened because we are Black, so we are not able to live to see this day, much less have the opportunity of living to see it. This was my WHY. It pains me to know that friends and my non-biological brothers and sisters across the border, lost their lives simply because of the colour of their skin, racism, and the fact that they did not get the opportunity to walk with me across that stage. I believe that education is a right, not a privilege and that my people ought to be treated with the greatest respect the moment they step across that stage.

When we participate in a Black graduation, the sense of unity that it brings to us resonates. Here we have the opportunity to speak with our elders and Black faculty members about what the real world holds for us when we graduate. This is an intimate ceremony and celebration for the Black community and Black graduates. AUSU virtually celebrated its third anniversary of Black Graduation this year and I have been approached to be one of the keynote speakers. My hope is that the legacy I established at this institution will last for many years to come and will serve as a model for other small colleges or universities in Canada to follow.

My degree was awarded with honours and the distinction Cum Laude. In my program, I was also the only Black female to receive the award of Excellence. The amount of pride I had for myself was so overwhelming. I just could not believe I had come so far. With all my efforts, I wanted to be an inspiration to someone and especially to those who look like me. The most important thing to me was to be satisfied with my accomplishments and to be proud of the woman I have become. As I now sit here, I have experience in politics, relationship building, community care, and leadership. Unexpected qualities and aspirations became part of my life that I did not realize was possible.

My education continued. Grad school was the next step, and I was accepted to Carleton University Master's program. Currently, I am studying at the Norman Paterson School of International Affairs, and I specialize in Health, Displacement, and Humanitarian Policy. It is a very competitive program that admits 250+ students per year. The joy that came with knowing
all my hard work paid off during my undergraduate program brought tears to my eyes. Rather than guidance counselors telling me I would not make it, I had advisors telling me the sky was the limit, keep going Pauline, we believe in you, and we know you will succeed if you work hard.

Throughout my undergrad, all I kept telling myself was, look how far you have come, you can do it, keep going. That being said, my goal is to work for Immigration, Refugees and Citizenship Canada. As my late grandfather did, one of my future goals is to work for the United Nations, specifically for the UNHCR- United Nations High Commissioner of Refugees. As a people person and someone who advocates for the wellbeing of humanity, I believe these are the best careers for me to pursue.

My grandfather, John Gampson Danquah, was one of five diplomats who were awarded the ALFRED NOBEL Peace Prize in 1981. He worked for the UNHCR as aforementioned. He was a member of the Group 5 that provided aid to refugees during the Ethiopian civil war. This was regarded as fundamental work for peace by the Nobel Committee. It was the UNHCR that was recognized as a lifetime achievement for their work in providing international protection to refugees in African, Asian, and Latin American countries. The prize motivation was "for promoting the fundamental rights of refugees."[1] I have never been so proud and honoured of anything as I am of being a member of a family that advocates for global human rights issues – as my grandfather did – and I am grateful for his support of human rights advocates everywhere. This is a message to my late grandfather:

Having the privilege of belonging to this family and knowing that my future aspirations come directly from your lineage is a blessing I cherish. Grandpa, I love you and I am so very proud of you. I wish I had the chance to grow with you and learn all the leadership qualities you once possessed. I know, though, that you are watching over me during every step I take on this academic journey. Thank you."

After writing my chapter, I realized that part of my pain was precisely the words my guidance counselor said to me when I was 17, that I would not be accepted to university based on my applied courses. But my confidence level grew to heights I never thought I would reach. My current position is not the result of my individual efforts, but rather through the combined power of prayer and faith in God, as well as having the unwavering support of my parents, my older sister, all my siblings, professors from undergrad as well as close friends. As a person on a journey of overcoming their pain, my advice is to always believe in yourself, set a goal in mind, and go for it. In addition, I am convinced that your age has no bearing on how successful you can be! Regardless of what someone says, never let their words hinder your efforts to achieve greatness.

Although words have the power to affect us, actions always speak louder! I am grateful for the obstacles that God put in front of me to make me who I am today and to appreciate the pain that led me to my purpose in life. Whether you believe in a higher power or not, focus on them for guidance because that is what keeps me going. As I am reminded by scripture that I always like to reference, success comes from God, and as I remain true to his word, I will always prosper.

1 Kings 2:3
And keep the charge of the Lord thy God, to walk in his ways, to keep his statutes, and his commandments, and his judgments, and his testimonies, as it is written in the law of Moses, that thou mayest prosper in all that thou doest, and whithersoever thou turnest thyself:

As I conclude, this is a special message for my Black Kings and Queens! We must continue to maintain our resilience and we must demonstrate to the world that Black lives will always matter and that we are not defined by negative stereotypes, especially when it comes to pursuing post-secondary education. Too often Blacks are stereotyped as only being talented in music, dance, sports, hair styling, or cooking. That is true, do not get me wrong, but that is NOT what we are limited to. Black people in professions such as medicine, education, law, politics, nursing, and engineering rarely receive notice for their success. The literature on Black inventors was nonexistent in my high school. The history of Black people has never been rooted in success, but rather in slavery.

Today, we are beginning to see a change, so keep pushing! Through my story, I want to encourage you to always aim for the stars, regardless of society's opinion of you. We are all unique and beautiful in our own way.

    I pray God's blessings on all of you who are reading my story. It is my hope that it resonated with you.

    1 Office of the United Nations High Commissioner for Refugees – Facts. NobelPrize.org. Nobel Media AB 2020. Sat. 21 Nov 2020. <https://www.nobelprize.org/prizes/peace/1981/refugees/facts/>

Pauline Danquah is passionate about her Christian faith, social justice, and human rights. You would normally find Pauline publicly speaking about the injustices mostly involving the lives of Black and marginalized people and the importance of having a spiritual connection with God.

Pauline is currently pursuing her master's degree at Carleton University with the Norman Paterson School of International Affairs. She aspires to work for the United Nations specifically the UNHCR.

Pauline enjoys the arts of cooking, hair styling, and the beauty of fashion! She is always ready for the camera!

Contact: pedanquah@gmail.com

https://www.facebook.com/paulineewuradjoa.danquah

52 Debra Wright

https://www.instagram.com/ladyp.xo/

5.

THE ROAD TO BECOMING A CITIZEN

Cindy Forbes

The journey of life can take you down many different paths. Some may take you away from those closest to you to pursue your own goals. Other times you are struggling to stay afloat, with your head barely above water. When trying to find your purpose and where you fit in, the path is never straightforward; there will always be challenges along the way. But, if you are walking on purpose, with a clear goal in mind, you are willing to push forward no matter the difficulty.

At seventeen years of age, I told myself that I would travel the world and make sure to take care of my family. However, I did not know what that would look like, living on the small island of Grenada. None of my family before me had ever left the island, and they were all comfortable without traveling. I, on the other hand, was desperate to get out and see the world. I kept my desire to travel to myself because I did not want to be laughed at and called a dreamer; also, there were no funds.

Just after my nineteenth birthday, I have presented the opportunity to travel abroad, and I readily agreed. I was contacted by a woman from my neighborhood who had moved to Canada. She was offering me an opportunity to work as a nanny. I took some time to process the information before I brought it to my parents, who were very accepting and gave me their blessing to travel. Even though my parents did not have a lot of money, they took out a loan to help me leave the island.

In the days following, I dealt with so many different emotions. I was scared because I had never left my island, and now I was about to venture off into this big world by myself. On the other hand, I was excited because my dream to travel was finally coming to pass, and in doing this, I would have better opportunities and get the chance to take care of my parents, even from a distance. On the day that I was leaving, there were a lot of tears. So many, in fact, that one of the airport personnel thought I would not pass the Canadian immigration and would be sent back to Grenada.

When I landed in Ontario, sure enough, she was right. The immigration officer asked me many questions to which I did not always have the answer. I was confused by the phrasing of the questions and became extremely nervous. I was escorted to an interview room, and by the time I completed the interview, then my passport and other document were taken from me. I was terrified. The officer then took me to a designated hotel for three days. It was the longest three days of my life.

I was angry with the situation because other immigrants, just like me, were seemingly having the time of their lives. It was almost as if they did not care about what would happen to them. Of course, anyone there would most likely be deported, but this did not phase them. On the other hand, I was concerned that I would be sent back to Grenada because I had come to Canada with a goal in mind, I had a purpose for being here, and the government could easily take away.

At the end of my three days, the woman who had contacted me about the nanny opportunity sent an immigration consultant to assist with my release. Unfortunately, upon my release, the immigration department never returned my documents to me. I was again concerned; this could impact my whole life because we need documentation for everything, and now I had nothing. I stayed with the woman and the family she was employed with for a few days, and I also visited a local church a couple of times before traveling to British Columbia.

I spent three years in British Columbia, and it wasn't enjoyable. The people that I was employed with treated me horribly, and I was always overworked. The pay did not add up to the amount of work and effort I was putting in. I cried many nights and even called my family in Grenada, begging them to come back home. Finally, one day the opportunity to go back to Ontario came up, and I discussed this with the family I was working with. They agreed that it would be best for me to go back to Ontario, they purchased my ticket, and I left, never looking back.

When I returned to Toronto, the church I had visited informed me that a family was looking for someone to watch their young children, and I agreed to take the position. I thoroughly enjoyed taking care of the children. Their mother and I became best friends, and eventually, I moved in with the family.

About a year later, I was still with the family, and we

discussed getting my permanent residence. I was motivated to do so after seeing everyone traveling abroad and coming back with stories on multiple occasions. However, it made me feel lonely and left out. I was disappointed with myself because I came to Canada with a purpose and could not fulfill it. I could not help my family let alone travel. I felt useless.

Shortly after our conversation, I began looking into applying for permanent residence and spoke with an immigration consultant. The paperwork was completed and submitted by the consultant. Unbeknownst to me, there was a warrant out for my arrest because I failed to show up at the immigration center before going to British Columbia. The consultant contacted me a few weeks later, advising me that I had an interview at the immigration center. I was under the impression that I was being approved. The consultant and I went together.

When I arrived at the immigration center, I was directed to an interview room, like the room when I first arrived in Canada. I began to panic a bit, remembering my first time at the immigration center. I was then informed that I could not leave the immigration center due to the warrant. I was overwhelmed with anxiety and upset with the consultant because he knew he could not help me; all he really did was take my money. He did not stay to help me process the information I had just received but instead kept looking at his watch, stating that he had another appointment, eventually leaving me to fend for myself. I felt extremely disrespected because he did not care about me. Finally, I was allowed to make a phone call and contacted my friend informing her of my situation. A few hours later, my friend posted my bond, and I met the immigration officer who handled my paperwork.

A lady who was also in the room with me looked at me and said, "you will be back." To which I promptly responded, "no, I will NOT be back," and left.

The condition for my release was that I checked in with immigration once a month. I did this for almost two years until I received a letter stating that I would be deported to Grenada. I was only given a week to pack my belongings and head to the airport where my ticket was waiting. This news was devastating because that meant leaving my Canadian family, along with all the hopes and dreams I had planned to accomplish here. The night before my flight, with my bags already packed, I suddenly declared, "I am NOT going anywhere."

The next morning, I went about life as normal, and this went on for weeks. No one came for me, no one called me, I did not even receive any letters. Finally, after a few years, I decided to reapply for permanent residence. I hired a lawyer, who informed me that I would need to reapply for my Grenadian passport before continuing the permanent resident process. I had more faith that I would be approved than my lawyer did. A few months later, I received a letter requesting my presence at an immigration center near me.

The immigration officer asked how I was doing, to which I stated that I was nervous. She then told me, "It's a beautiful day; you're getting your papers." I was completely shocked; I had no words. I made sure to get all my identification and immediately applied for school. This was an exciting time in my life. After all the struggles and setbacks, I was finally a resident of Canada. I felt like my life was back on track. I contacted my parents and let them know that I had recently become a resident of Canada and was now able to travel. I told them I would be coming for a visit sometime soon.

My first step was to get a job, and my journey began with applying for a Personal Support Worker course, which was six months in duration. Upon completion, I received my certificate and found a job shortly after. I worked as a Personal Support Worker for about a year before I took my first trip back to Grenada.

I was overjoyed knowing that I would see my family again and have the chance to spend time with them. I spent two weeks in Grenada, and when it was time to leave, it was a terribly sad moment. It brought me back to the very first time I left my island, and I cried. When I returned from my trip, I moved into my own apartment and decided to upgrade some of my credits to apply for the nursing program in college. I was accepted to college full-time and continued working as a casual Personal Support Worker (PSW).

When I had received my permanent residence papers, I was informed that I could apply for citizenship within two years because I had been in the immigration system for so long. Exactly two years later, I applied for my Canadian citizenship. I passed the citizenship test, and a few weeks later, I had my swear-in ceremony to become a Canadian citizen officially. I shared the good news with my family and friends. We celebrated with dinner.

Upon completing my nursing course, I obtained my

diploma as a Registered Practical Nurse and immediately received a job offer. I was excited because now I could really help take care of my family. The next item on my checklist was getting a vehicle because taking public transportation was an absolute nightmare, especially in winter. The very next year, I purchased my first vehicle, which allowed me to obtain a second job working as a Registered Practical Nurse in the community.

For the next few years, I worked and saved money to purchase a home of my own because I was tired of living in basement apartments. I also had the opportunity to go back to Grenada for the second time and spent two weeks with my family and friends.

When I returned from Grenada, I purchased my first home. I felt immensely proud of myself and accomplished. My journey to citizenship had been so long and strenuous, I had so many disappointments and setbacks, but here I was, a citizen, with my vehicle and home that I purchased with my own money by the grace of God. My dream to travel and help take care of my parents was now a true reality.

From the very beginning of my journey, I was always thinking of my family. This is what motivated me and kept me going. The family that took me in became my Canadian family, and with all that I endured, having them there to support me provided great comfort. The opportunities that I received in Canada I may not have had in Grenada. Becoming a nurse allowed me to grow into a leadership role as a preceptor, preparing student nurses for similar roles in the field. Working as a nurse in the community allowed me to connect with people from all walks of life and impact them in various ways. While talking to some of the clients in the community, I realized they were just as lonely as I had been many years prior. They just wanted someone to talk to, and I could be that listening ear and give encouragement when needed.

I know that when it came to my process with immigration, I was blessed to see it to completion because there were so many times that immigration could send me home, but God was always on my side, protecting me. As a result, I shared my story with my clients and, in addition, coworkers. I encouraged those in similar situations like myself and many others, encouraging them to persevere and never give up on their goals.

Whatever goal you set for yourself, there will always be hindrances along the way. You may be hurt, disappointed, feeling like you will never see the light at the end of the tunnel, or you may be alone with no support. But, no matter what it is, you can do it. Sometimes you must dig deeper within yourself to find the strength to carry on and push forward. Connect with someone who can encourage you to keep going. I found comfort in knowing I could turn to God whenever the situation looked bleak, but I also had friends and family to help me along.

I knew the goals I had as a seventeen-year-old could be attained, but I was unaware of the journey that laid before me. I walked many different paths, some more lonely and darker than others, but I kept walking, trusting that God would carry me through because I had a purpose. This was not just about me, but about my family as well. The desire to take care of them was so great that I had no choice but to keep my eyes forward and keep trekking.

Sometimes we lose our "why" amid the journey. When this happens, do not be afraid to step back and reevaluate where you are and where you want to go. This is your journey, and you are in control. Sometimes in the re-evaluation stage, you may find that your "why" has changed. As we get older and mature, some situations change us and how we perceive the world. For example, when I was being deported back to Grenada, I could have given up because I had no control over my immigration process. It would have been easier to leave because I would be with my family, and if I had, my journey would have changed completely. However, I remembered my "why" and stayed even though the odds were against me.

Remember that the journey of life has many roads that lead to your destination and purpose. Do not forget to celebrate the small wins along the way.

Cindy Forbes was born on one of the small islands in the Caribbean called Grenada, also known as the "Spice Isle." She is one of ten children born to her mother and father. At the age of 19, Cindy immigrated to Canada in search of a better life to help her family. In 2004 Cindy became a Personal Support Worker caring for the elderly. She then went back to college in 2006, where she graduated as a Registered Practical Nurse in 2008

Cindy is currently working with the elderly and holds a preceptor role mentoring nursing students, preparing them for the nursing field.

Contact: forbey31@hotmail.com

https://www.facebook.com/cindy.forbes.357

6.

JOURNEY FROM WITHIN

Rose M Young

Looking back, I sighed as I still have an evident memory of when it happened. It was April 4th, 2008, a wonderful sunny day. I was working in the Cardiac stress laboratory, and I remembered praying for the usually long workday to be done to complete my last patient's chart and be on my way to enjoying some of that beautiful weather. I was extremely excited and happy to be out of my tiny office.

I got my wish of finishing up before the sun was down, but what I certainly did not wish for is what happened after my shift was over.
Sometimes, it is best to travel the road less taken. Because I wanted to get home early, I decided to take the busy but fastest way, or so I thought at the time.

Less than ten minutes after work, I found myself in what I called "The Big Bang" of my life. I saw it coming, moving at an extremely rapid pace. I saw it coming from behind in the rear-view mirror seconds before it happened. All tensed up, I embraced myself for the impact as I saw my entire life flashed right in front of me. Bang! Bang! and Crash! Then in an instant, time stood still for what seems like an extremely long time, although it was only for a few minutes. Everything happened so fast. I closed my eyes then opened them again slowly.

The convoy of vehicles had come to a complete standstill. The beautiful sunlight was now outed by the many flashing lights of the emergency vehicles surrounding the cars involved, Ambulance, police cars, tow trucks, and fire trucks. It was like a scene straight out of a bad movie, and I was all caught up in it. The emergency assistance began to move faster and faster. In no time, everyone, including two small children, was transported in an ambulance and taken to the hospital nearby.

Luckily for me, I had no broken bones; however, I sustained many injuries to different parts of my body. Today, many years later, I am treated by a chiropractor because of the injuries I sustained from that day and another similar situation a few short years later.

My entire life was turned upside down, but I thanked God I could find my "Why." My "WHY" was the reason I needed to push forward. My "WHY" was my responsibility to fight harder than ever before to rise above it all. My children were and are still my "Why." Having a "WHY" will always help you to bounce back when life knocks you down. It will give you the drive you need to keep climbing.

Life knocked me down several times in very harshed ways, but God was always there to pull me back up again. To him, I give all the glory. Life can be rather confusing and challenging these days, especially with the coronavirus pandemic and our ever-changing world, but let us not dwelled on all the negatives. Instead, we need to focus on the understanding that change is vital and change is good.

It is also an incredible time in which we can grow and become transformed through much conclusive evidence. There are many successful stories of overcoming and becoming fulfilled and empowered even after traumatic or emotionally stressful situations, such as these on the pages of this book.

They testify to the fact there is purpose in all our pain. There is a purpose for us being here on this planet, and I believe that each of us is assigned different assignments to be completed while we are here. However, until we become fully aware, we will not fully understand what that assignment is.

The roadmap of my personal pain led me to find myself and realize my own truth. Through overwhelming and traumatic experiences of loss and pain resulting from not one but two life-changing multi-vehicle accidents, I struggled to overcome. Still, I also became empowered because of the many experiences from those hushed realities. I struggled to hold my head up about the deep depression I was once drowning in. I was hurting, not just from the physical or emotional pain, but I was also hurting spiritually to a point where I almost lost my entire self-value.

During that time of pain, losses and brokenness, I lost my esteem and self-confidence. I became a foreigner in an unknown and unfamiliar world. I did not like nor recognize the person looking back at me from a far distance in the mirror. I honestly became a stranger to myself. Because of the pain, I had also made many sense-less mistakes. It is quite easy to make very dumb mistakes when you are not aware of your innermost struggles. After years of many physical therapies and many hours of praying, and the quest of finding my way back, I learned to let it go. Through exceedingly difficult and testing times, I grew from the many personal experiences and lessons I have encountered on my very long journey back to a place of total awareness.

I was abandoned by many people I referred to by the famous word ***friends***; however, once they removed themselves, God sent others who prayed with me and motivated me to continue to push forward no matter how hard it was. And so, I did. How can you heal if you do not know how to cry? How can you become unbroken from your brokenness if you do not know how to forgive and love yourself? In my dark, deep, lonely state of brokenness and pain, I learned to love and forgive myself. Mostly, I learned to cry. I learned to let it all go. Many days I cried those ugly, loud and extra emotionally exhaling cries. I cried until I was all cried out.

Trust me when I say it was a relief to let those crystal raindrops of tears rain and fall where they wished. I felt free. Yes, it felt good!! The road of my pain led me here to a place where I can now use it to motivate and inspire you. It motivated me to find myself and find the confidence to move beyond the hard times and overcome the challenges I had to face. There was a time I was afraid I would venture into a very dark place inside. I became depressed and was afraid of going to a place of no return, yet I courageously stared fear in the eyes. For what were my choices then? I now know that fear was an obstacle that wanted to keep me stuck.

Sometimes we tend to forget that we are never alone;

God is with us, always. I also understood that situations could either be completely good, bad, or not so bad. It is all about how we interpret it. It is also about how the viewer views each situation. During those confusing times, I interpreted my situation as bad; crying did not make the pain go away but after a good cry. I felt better.

It is an amazing feeling when your heart, mind, soul, and entire body are free. Go ahead cry if you must. Free yourself of all the tension and stress of your past broken trust. Forgive yourself and render love to those who contributed to your pain. Forgive them and let that ray of sunshine in so God can begin to use you in a mighty good way. You deserve a life of fun, laughter, love and absolute abundance. Think, speak and live what you believe is true for your own life. Remember, what others are thinking about you is none of your prerogatives. God loves you. I knew that God loved me, and that was good enough for me. I also grew to love myself, and that is what matters most. Always keep in mind that it is about you and your creator.

Sometimes you may be feeling stuck and desperate, but it is in those defining moments of ultimate discomfort, desperation, and brokenness that you can find yourself and your greatest strength. Through many dark and heavy downpours of crystal teardrops, I found my beautiful rainbow, a meaningful life that I can now appreciate. I know now that there was a purpose for all my pain. Gaining control of my inner thoughts also helped me view the situation from a different perspective. As a result, I was optimistic about my future as I began to think from the end. I saw myself happy; I saw myself confident; I saw myself pain-free. I saw myself fully transformed and healed.

Having a positive attitude to whatever is happening in your life is an incredible remedy to your inner healing, which will heal your outer physical self. Of course, you will sometimes have situations or even other people who will challenge you. However, if you acknowledged that they are stressors and are there to test you, you will be able to redirect your thoughts and emotions to other things and positive people. Focus on feeling victorious and only engage in activities that will give you positive feedback. Traveling within and finding myself took confidence, courage, and time. As I mentioned before about the different stressors and challenges, I have had my share of such. There was a time, not too long ago, when one such individual tested me. I had to revisit my thoughts. A positive attitude and a positive mindset helped me forgive this person for that challenge and broken trust.

It was hard, but I needed to reconnect to my inner being, which I called "self." The brokenness from someone you consider a friend can hurt as bad or sometimes even worse than the physical pain of an accident. To be emotionally or spiritually broken is just as painful and may leave lifelong scars that could affect you for years to come. However, when we are aware of our thoughts and know-how to live our life from within, it is much easier to heal from the things that the outside world throws at us. The decision is usually up to us on how we choose to handle each situation. I thank God for the journey. It has been and still is an incredible one. And, as I continue my inner life's journey, my purpose is becoming clearer and clearer each day.

I encourage you to have faith and believe that after the storm, there will always be calm. It may seem like an exceptionally long time, but also trust that it will not be forever. As the saying goes, "Nothing lasts forever." Love yourself even when you feel like giving up. Remember that love is precious, delicate, and should be nurtured. Love is what keeps us going and gives us hope. Loving yourself from within and loving others is the only practical way to become heal and fulfilled. With struggles comes many hidden treasures, but it is up to everyone to find those beautiful treasures buried deep within.

Our struggles can either make us or break us. After the second accident happened, I could have easily given up. Yet, I learned to turn down the noises of distractions, discouragement, confusion, and the noise of every pain, every ache, and every tingling and numbness in my body that told me I should. I learned to drown out the many opinions from people that told me I needed back surgery. I drowned out all the negativities. Once you shut off all the different noises around you, allow yourself to be still, become one with your entire being, body, soul, and mind. There you will find your peace.

Someone asked me once about what I wanted; to them, I say peace. *When you have peace in this life, you have everything.* Your purpose will pursue you. Your abundance will be endless, and happiness becomes not a wish but rather a beautiful lifestyle of how our creator intended our lives to be. Believe in the beautiful evolution of your growth. When the pain becomes unbearable, and there seems to be no hope, think from the end. Find the bridge between your now and your after.

Think of the possibilities of what could be possible in your future if you could push through the aches, the distractions, and the anxiety no matter what the situation looks like. Be the best you can be and face each waking day with great expectations. Say you will; believe you will, and you will overcome. Know that something extraordinary will happen for someone in this world, because of your struggles and because of your pain. You are bigger than your present. In times to come, your pain will unselfishly help someone else to mend their brokenness. It may not seem that way now, but also know that there are appreciations found in the core of the hardships encountered. As I worked on my inside, I became inspired, knowing that God would see me through.

When I asked God to take control, he took control, and in return, he gave me blessings. He gave me hope, and he gave me another chance to fulfill my divine destiny. When you put your trust in the creator, he will make you master of your own evolution. He will help you to create a new story that is yet to be told. Imagine creating your story, and you are the star and hero of your own story. I believe that mindfulness and the roots of where your inner pain is coming from can help us better understand what action is needed to help us with our present emotions. Knowing the origin of your growing pain is key to eliminating the triggers.

I encourage you to embrace the struggles of your pain and take back control of what you dream of becoming. Grab the bull by the horn, so to speak. Find out what is the connection between your present struggles and your past. Then rewrite the story you want. Yes, life is a journey, but it is important to know your true journey begins from within. Do not be a stranger to yourself and never leave yourself behind. Have faith; your future blessings are greater than your past experiences.

Rose Marie Young is an Empowerment Trauma Life Coach who is currently residing in the beautiful province of Ontario Canada. She is an inspirational entrepreneur with a passion for helping others in all areas of their lives. She is an International Best-Seller Author and compiler of the Broken Trust anthology on Amazon.Com.

She is also an active member of Destiny Coaching Group and an affiliate of America's Number one Best Confidence Coach, Dr. Keith Johnson. Rose studied and completed an academic program at 83K Academy where she obtained her certifications in Church Growth Coaching, Leadership Coaching, Life Coaching, and Business Coaching. She is also a writer and speaker with a certification in Mindfulness Coaching as well.

Rose is considered a master coach in the coaching and consulting industry. Rose Marie Young worked in the health field for many years before changing to her new career choice. She worked as a health care worker part-time and as a Certified Cardiology Technologist full-time.

Rose is a lover of nature who enjoys the outdoors life and is an embassy for health and wellness. She constantly thrives for inner growth, and it's her God-given purpose to help empower others.

Contact: rmarie1695@gmail.com

https://www.instagram.com/rose.marie.young/

https://www.facebook.com/rose.young.902

Website: https://rosemarieyoung.com/

7.

PURPOSE FUELED THROUGH PAIN

Marlene Mae Henry

For I know the plans I have for you," declares the Lord, "plans to prosper you and not to harm you, plans to give you hope and a future. (Jer. 29:11)

My existence in this world came through the struggle and tension of a very young woman who became impregnated by a much older man. The decision whether to abort her baby or to bear the shame of having yet another child out of wedlock. My mom chose the former. Thus, I dedicate this chapter to my mother, whom I emulate in personality and character. My mom's disposition and deportment are seen as someone with determination, courage, faithfulness, and love for her family and community. These attributes serve as a testimony to who I have developed to be.

When I think about my recent achievement, having graduated with a Master of Theological Studies, my mind goes back to where my academic journey began. It spawned out with a painful experience when my marriage ended, and this forced me out of my comfort zone into the unknown. Although I must admit, I love order, structure, predictability, and my reaction to chaos induces my stress level as I do not gravitate to change easily. And to have my world as I know, it turned upside down was traumatic, to say the least.

When I think about the theme "No pain, no gain," It connects me with my own experiences dealing with pain where I have found that in the painful experience, I was forced to not only wrestle with my emotions but also gained the strength and inspiration through thoughtfulness, prayer, and strategic planning, refocusing my energy into forging a pathway to working on my next goal. Not because I did not pray hard enough, fasted long enough, or exercised more faith. Before I could process what was happening, I found myself alone, and it took a couple of days for me to process the finality of the situation. When the reality hit me that I was really deserted, and the marriage I held sacred was truly over, my heart ached within me. The pain intensified every time I thought about my pitiful situation.

Over the coming weeks, I suffered more internally. I lost my appetite for any form of food, my limbs felt like jelly, I had problems concentrating as my thoughts would wander off. I often felt like I did not want to get out of bed as life became mundane. How ironic that one of my comforting thought was to return to Jamaica to my mom, who, by the way, I did not tell of what was going on in my life at that time. It was also during the time that I had returned to school for the 2-year college study program. I felt I could not go on for days, but I was encouraged to redirect my pain into something meaningful. And I thought that if nothing else can work, studying may be the answer. So, I immersed myself in my study, and for two years, college life became my life. In volunteering as a student ambassador, a student mentor taking on five protégés, and with being employed at the Student Life center assigned to mostly the international students, I was able to challenge my energy into something meaningful for myself.

I was able to share my story within the narratives of many of my assignments. In addition, I was also a part of the cross-border project group to Jamaica as an internship student. This provided me with meaningful experiences that led to various opportunities to serve within the community at the local, regional, and international levels. At the end of my study, I graduated with honors and was awarded the "Leader by Example and Student Mentorship in Life and Education" awards. How did I achieve this? By redirecting my pain into specific goals, I wanted to accomplish. I was purposeful to finish my college study, but it was a step-by-step process.

First, it propelled me to return to school where I acquired a college diploma; then, I moved on to gain a Bachelor of Arts in Community Development, then I pursued a master's degree in Theological studies. All of which was a result of turning pain into purpose! Looking back now at my college experience, it took all that I knew that was inside me learning from my mom. I remember reflecting on how I would see my mother react when faced with a challenge, and something like determination would often stir up within me. I would repeatedly pray and encourage myself over and over again, "Lord, even though I don't see or feel you, as long as you have not left me, I am trusting you."

However, before leaving college, my professor challenged me to further my studies at the undergrad level. This would attract even greater challenges as I would have to relocate to another city and away from my family, community connections, and networks. But, having decided to do a leap of faith, I took the plunge. This move was not an easy one. I found that studying in a strange environment was both exciting and perplexing. For one thing, the climate was precarious and having to endure extreme winter months, feeling of isolation from one's own culture required physical and emotional endurance. For example, I remembered on a frigid and icy Saturday morning going to the university to study and missing the bus. This was where I found out that this city was a car and truck culture. The public transit runs on an hourly timeframe on weekends.

I have never experienced such cold as I stood in the open range waiting for the next bus to arrive. I kept telling myself as my brain felt like it was gradually shrinking, I felt disorientation from being exposed to the cold. In addition, my patience slowly eroding "the bus will be here soon," as tears began to swell and feelings of frustration increased. I began to cry, and between tears, I remembered arguing with God about the lesson behind my present suffering as even the element was against me. But no answer came, as the seconds moved to minutes and the hour seem like an eternity before the bus arrived.

My studying experience started with tension. I learned in wrestling with my emotions how to distinguish between what is comfortable for me in the present compared to what will be best for me in the future through endurance. I learn another valuable lesson: pain is temporary, but the lesson gained in the experience is long-lasting. I needed to adapt to a new environment, a new way of life to survive the present experience. Now, I have adapted to this new way of life and made the north my permanent home. The lesson gained; a painful experience may often become a process to which something greater can emerge. Hence, after graduating with my undergrad with high honors, the culmination of my masters.

This is where all the painful experiences began to make sense to me. The mission and ministry that I am called to require that to serve effectively and to develop empathy, I had to have gone through some struggles of my own. As I recall, I was able to pull from some of my own experiences to give real context to the topics of discussions. This added substance and helped shape my understanding of the solidification of the pedagogical approach to both the theological and praxis of my academic experience.

What did I learn?

Going back to college made me realize that going through a painful experience is not the end, but as I reached out for help, I got support from family, friends, and community; I could re-channel my pain into something with a personal determination more meaningful. Having achieved one goal gave me more fuel to go on to the next goal, which was to further my education. This was required for the next level of my academic life as to the purpose and reason behind my passion and focus for supporting marginalized people through the Ideology, theology, and praxis lens.

So, with clarity, I recall my personal, family, and church relationships, not only my interactions dealing with vulnerability, enduring suffering, loss, and pain, and my experience with rejection. But I was able to recall times where joyful moments were felt when prayers were answered, the celebration of achievement to memorialize various accomplishments and funny stories that brought laughter even to tears.

So, as I reflect on my life's journey on what gave my painful experience the fuel it needed, my mother's passion, love, and dedication gave me the determination never to give up. She instilled within me an attitude of humility to acknowledge what I am going through and never give in to negative feelings. That faith in God even when I do not understand what He is doing, but by remaining faithful, humble, and thankful, God will bring out His purpose for the experience whether sad or joyful, negative, or positive, God is in control. I thank, appreciate, and love my mom for her sacrifice, and she is one of the mentors that I can gain wisdom, especially if I must make some major decisions.

Now I know what my mom meant when she said to my father, "I want my baby." I believe that I am in this world for a reason, and although some of the experiences are very painful, they serve a higher purpose. The reason for the experience begins to come to light. For example, I am personally dealing with type-2 diabetes and hypotension and struggles with my faith in seeking healing for these health challenges. However, I can realize that it was not God's will that I will be healed. To understand more about my health issues and help others, I signed up and became a Community Diabetes Awareness Ambassador. I learned I could take it back to my community and raise awareness of possible detection and treatment when dealing with type-two diabetes. The overall purpose became clearer to me.

This was to facilitate various information sessions to

local church groups, local community colleges, and the Universities. I raised the subject through group work projects and advocacy, among other social burdens. This included the increased financial cost as the health factors for students upon graduation in developing diabetes due to precarious diet and eating habits. I was living with both of these experiences myself.

Based on everything I went through, I believe that regardless of the painful situation we find ourselves in, there is always hope and light at the end of the tunnel. The situation might appear to belong and be drawn out, and there seems to be no end in sight, but from my experience dealing with pain, it has and will come to pass. So, I chose to believe that Joy does come in the morning. Let the purpose unfold!

In 2008, Marlene founded Helping -Hands International Canada as she believes that the holistic approach to community advocacy and capacity building is best supported through awareness, education, and counseling.

Marlene has a Diploma in Social Service work with Honors (Seneca College); B. A cum laude.
Community Development (Algoma University); and a master's degree in Theological Studies (Tyndale University & Seminary). Marlene is also an International Best-Selling author.

Contact: mmaehenry@gmail.com

https://www.facebook.com/mmaehenry

https://www.instagram.com/marlene9127/

8.

THE PURSUIT OF PURPOSE

Glen Prince

The greatest tragedy is not death, but life without purpose
  – Rick Warren

It would be almost impossible to talk about the "Pursuit of Purpose" from a Christian perspective without including King David in the discussion. One day, according to 1 Samuel, the 16th chapter, the prophet Samuel showed up in Bethlehem with the intent of anointing one of Jesse's eight sons as King, who would one day, at God's choosing, replace the current king, King Saul.

The setting is one of great intrigue. The announcement that Prophet Samuel, who was considered the mouthpiece of God, was coming to Bethlehem brought some uneasiness in the city since the prophet was the one with the assignment to pronounce God's judgment when necessary.

1 Samuel 16:4b-5 "And the elders of the town trembled at his coming, and said, Comest thou peaceably? And he said, peaceably: I am come to sacrifice unto the Lord: sanctify yourself and come with me to the sacrifice. And he sanctified Jesse and his sons and called them to the sacrifice."

The intrigue continued as Jesse showed up to the sacrifice with only seven of his eight sons. The prophet apparently did not know how many sons Jesse had and did not take the time to count. The culture of the time stressed that the first-born son had certain privileges in what I call "the-next-in-line system." The prophet Samuel looked at Eliab and proclaimed, *"surely the Lord's anointed is before me. "(I Samuel 16:6)* and would have anointed him, king, had not God intervened, *"...Look not on his countenance, or the height of his stature; because I have refused him: for the Lord seeth not as man seeth: for man looketh on the outward appearance, but the Lord looketh on the heart." (1 Samuel 16:7)* The truth is: the two ways you can promote a person is legally or illegally. The first can only be achieved by the preordained plans and purposes of God. You can achieve the second by not having an ear to God and ignoring all the signals he sends your way.

The first son, Eliab, no doubt looked the part but based on the rebuke that the Lord gave, looking the part was not good enough. However, Jesse was unmoved; he was apparently determined to ensure that the next King came from his house.
1 Samuel 16:8-10 "Then Jesse called Abinadab and made him pass before Samuel. And he said, neither hath the Lord chosen this. Then Jesse made Shammah pass by. And he said, neither hath the Lord chosen this. Again, Jesse made seven of his sons pass before Samuel. And Samuel said unto Jesse. The Lord hath not chosen these.

At this point, I would imagine that the prophet was undeniably frustrated. He had walked with God for a long time, even from the time when God spoke to him in Eli's temple as a little boy, and he knew that God would not send him to this specific house in this specific city unless there were a king there to be anointed.

I Samuel 16:11 "And Samuel said unto Jesse, Are here all thy children? And he said, There remaineth yet the youngest, and behold; he keepeth the sheep. And Samuel said unto Jesse, Send and fetch him: for we will not sit down till he comes hither."

Jesse's response to Samuel's question cannot and should not be glossed over. The prophet of God left his house in Ramah and traveled to Bethlehem to your specific house with a horn of oil in his hand and clear authority and instruction from God to anoint a king. So why would you not bring all your sons to the sacrifice? Could it be based on a tradition that David, being the youngest, would not become King ahead of his bothers? Whatever the reason, someone reading this portion of scripture must understand that the "oil" of God will pursue and find you wherever you are.

When David was located, no doubt in some obscure place on the backside of a mountain, he did not have time to wash up, nor did he have time to prepare himself to go before the prophet as his brothers did – he came as he was.

1 Samuel 16:12-13 "... Now he was ruddy and withal, of a beautiful countenance, and goodly to look to. And the Lord said, Arise, anoint him: for this is he. So then Samuel took the horn of oil and anointed him in the midst of his brethren: and the Spirit of the Lord came upon David from that day forward."

The purpose is defined as "the reason why something is done or used. Further, it's the aim or intention of something: it evokes a feeling of being determined to do or achieve something". Purpose is similar to potential: It speaks to all that you can be but has not yet become. It speaks to how far you can go but have not yet gone. Unless the purpose is pursued, it remains, like potential, untapped. Like the diamond deep in the earth, the beauty and joy you created to bring to the earth remain unrealized.

My name is Glen Prince. I was born in a small village in San Juan, Trinidad, located on the Eastern side of the country, a few miles off the East-West Corridor just before the Santa Cruz Valley. I received my elementary education at Bourg Mulattress RC School, attended Aranguez Secondary School for my junior years, and the San Juan Senior Comprehensive for my high school years, brand new at the time. I wasn't a standout student; I struggled through with average grades. I had decided and still believe that all my teachers hated me; my twin brother Glenroy and my youngest sister Bernadette were the ones who made consistently good grades, while I remained the child who was always in trouble, both in school and the neighborhood. In those bygone days, corporal punishment (beatings) was legal and encouraged by my parents, so my butt was probably beaten every day. If not, surely every other day.

My parents, Godwin and Beatrice, were never married but lived in what was commonly known as a "common-law relationship," which Church Folks will call "shacking up." My seven siblings and I all carried my mother's last name, Prince, while my father was Alexander. They had both emigrated from the island of Grenada and had put down stakes in Febeau Village. They weren't well-educated by world standards, but they instilled in us a sense of respect and pride as far back as I can recall. We were very poor, but we never knew it. My mother exuded excellence. She never missed an opportunity to entertain, always breaking out her "fine china" – that was off-limits for everyday use – when there was to be "company," which we would often tease her about. My father worked with the government, building schools, and other government buildings, while my mother worked as domesticated help, cleaning the homes of the elites.

As far back as I could remember, I would have dreams about things happening or getting ready to happen in our community. I would see things in visions that I was unable to explain sensibly. I always had a sense that I was going to do something great on the earth. I could not explain it since I really didn't know anyone at that time who was doing anything that I would have wanted to emulate, but there was a fire burning in my belly that seemed almost to propel me forward.

In 1983, I began making plans to migrate to the United States. My aunt Agatha, my mother's sister, had lived in the United States since the early 1970s, and she swore that the "States is where you need to be." With her encouragement, I began to dream of living in the United States, and after talking with my parents (well, mainly my mother), I decided to migrate to the US. This decision completely changed my life as I began to feel a force that I cannot explain, pulling me towards the day I would leave the shores of Trinidad and Tobago and step on the shores of the United States.

With the help of my mother, I booked a flight on Pan Am Airlines to travel to the United States on January 31st,

1984, less than a week shy of my 19th birthday. The problem was that I had not yet secured a Visa from the US Embassy. Nonetheless, I purchased a red and gray suitcase, began to say farewell to friends and family, and even had a farewell party. Still, I didn't yet have the Visa to travel.

I needed two things to secure my Visa: (1) an invitation letter from someone in the United States inviting me to come for a visit and (2) a financial statement from someone in Trinidad showing that they had the financial resources to care for me during my travels. Unfortunately, although I had the letter, the financial statement was elusive because my parents did not have any money in the bank even to get such a statement.

Less than a week before my departure, the Lord sent an angel: a friend of my mother. The friend gave me a financial statement, and a few days before my scheduled departure, I walked into the Embassy and was granted my Visa. Nevertheless, the force or the hand of God continued to be heavy on me. The best description of this force was that, in me, there was a knowing that I was not in control of my destiny. I felt assured that while I was leaving all that I had ever known, like Abraham, who in the book of Genesis was commanded, *"Get thee out of thy country, and from thy kindred, and thy father's house, unto a land that I will show thee."* (Genesis 12:1), God was leading me towards my divine destiny. The strange thing is that he didn't say it in audible words, nor did He show it to me in a vision. Instead, there was a knowing deep down inside that I was being led by the invisible hand of God.

On January 31st, 1984, I landed at John F. Kennedy International Airport in New York City, scared and cold.

It was the dead of winter, and I didn't travel with a coat. It would turn out that the person who was supposed to meet me with a coat, my aunt, never showed up to the airport, almost as if she thought that I wasn't going to be allowed entry. However, as I approached the Customs Officer who would decide if I would be allowed entry into the United States or not, there was a peace that overtook me; truthfully, I thought that the hard part was behind me, and this guy would stamp my passport and allow me to enter. Instead, he asked, "Who will you be staying with?" I responded, "My aunt." He asked, "Where does your aunt live?" I responded, "737 West 14th Street in Manhattan." He looked at me, and in my youthful ignorance, I looked back at him. "Why are you coming to the United States?" he asked. I responded, "To attend a wedding." He responded, "Let me see the invitation," which I proceeded to hand to him.

He looked at it, then looked back at me and said, "You know there is no wedding, right?" For the first time, I felt fear; in my mind's eye, I began to picture this guy refusing me entrance and sending me back to Trinidad. I saw me pulling that red and gray suitcase through the neighborhood and all the neighbors looking at me, mocking me for my failure.

It was similar to those old Western movies that I watched as a child where two-gun slingers stared down at each other before drawing their guns and shooting. The Customs Officer stood there staring at me as his words lingered in the atmosphere. Not knowing what to do, I stared right back at him, dreading the thought of pulling that red and gray suitcase through my old neighborhood. Finally, in what seemed like a lifetime, he dropped the invitation letter he was holding. He picked up his stamp, stamped my passport, and handed it back to me along with the letter. He proceeded to say, "You are lucky I have a heart." And with those words, I entered the United States with that fire raging inside of me.

Thirty-seven years later, I sit here penning these words that I pray will inspire someone who reads it to understand that purpose is elusive. It does not sit on a shelf where one can easily reach up and grab it down, but you must pursue it. I've had many struggles: the aunt who wanted me to come to the United States mistreated me beyond words, causing me almost to become homeless; I slept around, changing mates and smoking weed; I even owned a nightclub. These were all things that I had never learned from my parents, nor was I taught them in my upbringing. But the fire that churned in my belly as a boy never went out.

Today, I am saved, married with three children, living a fulfilled life in the suburbs of Chicago. I am the Senior Pastor of a ministry that my wife and I birthed called Ruach Ministries. I am a published author (The Birth of a Vision), serving in the five-fold as an Apostle and holding an M.Div. I have traveled the world as far away as India and South America.

The portion of scripture that motivates me the most as I pursue the purpose that God has placed in me is Psalm 139: in it, David says of God:

Psalm 139:13 – 16 "For thou hast possessed my reins: thou hast covered me in my mother's womb. I will praise thee: for I am fearfully and wonderfully made, marvelous are thy works, and that my soul knoweth right well. When

I was made in secret, my substance was not hidden from thee and curiously wrought in the lowest parts of the earth. Thine eyes did see my substance, yet being unperfect, and in thy book, all my members were written...."

I have learned over the years that purpose is not something that you create in your own strength or intellectual acumen, but it's instead something that you discover as you trust and submit to a God who is full of abilities. My mistakes and stumbles were me discovering my purpose, and they certainly did not disqualify me from the greatness that was placed in me at birth. So often, I find myself alone, sitting on a plane or in the car heading out on an assignment, and I will say to myself, "Ms. Beatrice's son, you have come a long way." I smile and look around, making sure no one has seen me and labeled me as being crazy. I then remind myself, "You still have ways to go." Clearly, the joy of treasure hunting is unsure of what you will find, but when God created you and me, he placed the treasure inside of us.

Boldly declaring the Word of God, Apostle Prince is an in-demand preacher, teacher, and counselor to Pastors and other leaders across the globe. A native of Trinidad and Tobago, Apostle Prince, accepted the call upon his life to reach the nations and has traveled extensively in the United States, India, the Western Hemisphere, the Caribbean, and South America.

His ministry is marked by prophetic accuracy with an unwavering desire to see the lost saved, healed, delivered, and set free.

Apostle Prince is the Senior Leader of Ruach Ministries in Elgin, IL. He holds a master's degree in Theology and is currently working on an additional degree in Psychology and Counseling. He is also the author of "The Birth of a Vision."

Apostle Prince is married to Charlene Prince, who serves alongside him in ministry, and together they have three children. He constantly encourages his family to reach for greatness.

Contact: gjprince112@gmail.com

https://www.facebook.com/apostleglen.prince

9.
LETTING GO
Anna Pereira

What does it mean to push past the pain? It can mean many different things to different people. For me, it means to survive in a world that sometimes does not always work out the way we planned it.

In that case, pain, I believe, is a loss, a loss of something or someone that you hold so near and dear to you, with the mere thought of losing that one thing or that one person would hurt so badly that you would not be able to breathe.

I realized throughout my life that to be growing; there were times that I had to cross through the trenches of pain. Sometimes I had company, and other times I did not. I walked through many long and painful roads of self-doubt and often wondered where life was taking me. I was desperate to reach the warm sunrise of my divine purpose. But, do I even have a divine purpose? And if so, how do I know what it is? Will I know once I find it? These are all questions I asked and wanted to figure out.

Today I recognize that as awful and hurtful those days were in my life, there was a sense of purpose for what I was going through. You never really see it at the time it is happening, but there is always a purpose. Did I like it?

Heck no, I do not believe anyone can say that they enjoyed it during their painful moments of life. But, I can say that these moments in my life shaped me, and they certainly made me the strong and independent woman I am today.

Throughout my journey, I have to say that I met so many wonderful kindred souls. I would not have believed it back then, but I am telling you that God always knows what he is doing. I believe that God never leaves us with a task without sending out a few lifelines if we get stuck along the way. He definitely sent me some wonderful lifelines of my own, both male and female. I am confident that during your dark and painful moments, if you sit still enough and listen, your lifelines are there too. Some of my lifelines are still present in my life today, while others I have released and mourned their loss.

I have had many trials that brought me to my knees throughout my life. Looking back, this would be one of the most profound times of my life that I feel compelled to share with you in hopes that it will provide some hope of pushing through the pain. I have lost in love, but along with that was the closest chance I had to become a mother. I had people taunt me about it; some mocked me, while others full out laughed directly in my face that my dreams were falling apart.

At that time, I was raging and wanted those people to suffer like I was. It was not right, but I was hurting like never before. I was already over 40 years of age, and I was mentally prepared, and my body was physically ready; however, God was not ready to give me what I longed for. You may hear people say that it is not in God's plan. Well, for me, hearing that set me off like a firecracker. What about my plan? I had a plan; I was going to get married and have babies. That was my plan; why can't I have it the way I want it? Will it ever be in my future?

I am not sure, but that mustard seed of hope and faith still prevails onward today. I can tell you it took me years to be okay with saying that the master's plan is always the best.

Having come to terms with the thought that I would never be a mother was hard for me. It is a painful experience; It is the kind of pain only the inner you will know its depths. It is not visible to the outside world because you guard it so much. The kind that is crushing you and making every step you take feel like your feet are stuck in the mud. The kind that takes control over your every thought compelling you to be completely absorbed by it. I hid it well from everyone because I did not want to be falling apart all the time. Feeling like I was a burden to my family and friends for always longing for something I did not have.

Be happy, they would say, be strong, be independent, who needs a man they would say, you do not need to be a mother. They preached so many adages to me I got sick of hearing them. I started to tune people out and smile and nod. I would make excuses just so I did not have to be around people that drove me insane with the phrases of, you are better off on your own anyway, being a mother is hard work, and you will not be able to keep up with them at your age. It all left me feeling worse than before I arrived for a visit. Sometimes I would spend time with individuals who had children and left feeling torn. I was so upset that they did not truly hear me. They assumed that they knew what I was feeling and did not really listen to my situation.

Sometimes all I wanted was someone to listen to me and validate the pain I was going through. They had no clue I was dealing with the kind of pain that can make you cry for days. The kind that makes your body ache, the kind that takes away your will to smile. That is the pain I was dealing with, and it took me years to release that anger and pain. I pushed through those days one day at a time, planting a smile on my face for the outside world to see, while on the inside, I was broken, literally dying.

My father once told me that if I let things consume me, I will miss living my life and that the years will pass, and I will be left behind. Only God knows what is for you, he would say. Such a wise man, he absolutely knows that being angry about your loss keeps you stuck in life. So stuck that we sometimes miss the lessons. At the time, my thoughts on my father's advice were, "what is he talking about?" Unfortunately, I am having a crisis over here! I do not have time to dissect what God is trying to teach me or, for that matter, keep me from. I do not have the capacity to decipher what I am supposed to be learning from these lessons, and I am in too much pain. I felt like I was dying a thousand deaths, with each one worse than the last.

I knew time was running out on my hopes and dreams of becoming a mother. I was ready to deal with the loss of my relationship, but I was not ready to deal with the loss of becoming a mother. But, no way was I going to give up! I prayed and prayed; I made promises to God; I was fervent in my prayers. I joined worship groups, started hanging out with prayer warriors, pleading to anyone who would listen, thinking they had a direct line to God. I was already what I considered a devoted catholic and belonged to a ministry within my church. I was trying to prove to God that I was a good person and do whatever was needed to be a mother if he would grant me that one thing in life. A task that eventually took its toll on me mentally.

I was often invited to go to baby showers and baptisms and even birthday parties throughout this ordeal. Inside I was holding it together as tightly as I could, knowing at any minute it could unravel if my mind started to wonder. I was asked to hold these babies, so I would silently cry on the inside, thinking that it felt like torture to be holding any baby when I was desperate for one of my own. Do not get me wrong, I love holding babies, but it was like someone just punched me in the gut without warning.

Several years passed, and I was presented with yet another situation that brought much pain. I lost a dear friend to cancer. While it was sudden, he was also devoted. I had just met him, but we connected spiritually, and we had some profound talks about God. During one of our talks, we spoke about the paths we take in life and that sometimes we are given paths that serve a higher purpose. He would tell me that we never know the purpose; we must have faith like a mustard seed. I would argue with him on that and tell him my faith was running on empty lately.

I really enjoyed our talks, and on Sundays, I would often speak to him coming and going from church. He was a humorous guy, always making me laugh whenever we talked. We talked about specific hymnal songs we enjoyed; with me being part of the Church choir, it came up often. I would share the songs I enjoyed with him, and he would share with me the hymns he loved to sing. He had a great voice, but I could never get him to join the choir.

Soon after I met him, he was hospitalized and about a week later passed away. In his honor, we sang his favorite song at his funeral. It was hard to be strong and hold back the tears as we sang with so much love for him and his precious life. I will never forget the song that he loved, which reminds me of him, and that day I was given a spiritual message from above.

During one of my dark days of being in so much pain, I started screaming at God. I was getting ready for Church crying hysterically and screaming at God why I was so behind in life. I felt like I was not where I was supposed to be. I went down the path of disbelief, a path I stumble across every so often in my life. So, with a mounting point of disbelief, I became more and more angry, feeling helpless, defeated, and cheated by life, with the added emotional strain that I knew was fast approaching. I started to call on my friend, saying if there is a heaven and if God is so real, let me know by playing your favorite song in church today. Yes, I was testing God once again and in so much pain. I was so done with the world and with believing in God that I was grasping onto straws. Looking for the slightest bit of hope to hang onto. There had to be more than just this life of pain for me; I could not for one minute believe that this was it.

After cleaning my face and reapplying my makeup to head out to church, I put that conversation away and did not think of it until much later during mass.

Usually, once a week, we would practice the songs for the upcoming Sunday mass. We always knew what we were singing for the most part before Sunday. Albeit there were some changes as we went along but nothing out of the ordinary Sunday hymnal songs. It was probably the 3rd or 4th song that I was in disbelief...The morning rant that I had with God and my friend came flooding back to me and filled my eyes with tears. I was shocked that the very song that I asked my friend to make us sing was being sung. That song is never played on Sunday; it is commonly sung at funerals. As I sat and cried in the middle of my choir, my choir members around me started one by one, placing their hands on my upper shoulders as a sign that they were there for me, showing me compassion at a time when I was so fragile.

Finally, with tears streaming down my face and hearing them splatter onto the pages of the hymnal book, I got up and mustered up the energy to sing the last 2 verses. Frankly, my perspective changed that day, believing that there is a God and that heaven is a real thing. Receiving the sign that he has me and he has all my troubles, and although I am in pain, and although I have had many painful days in my life, he is very much alive and present in my life.

So, now and again, when I get a little down at not being gifted with the title of motherhood, I do not push away the pain. I do not resist it, I almost picture it as a thought that is allowed into my mind, but I do not permit it to stay there for long. I accept it as part of my path; I do not get stuck there. It may take a day or two to process my feelings and the emotions that come from them. What I have learned to do is to plan a day to nurture myself to feel better.

Sometimes it is as simple as staying home, making popcorn, and watching movies that make me laugh. Other times it is making my favorite meal or just pampering myself with a spa day, taking long drives in the fall to take in the beauty of nature. I honor the pain, recognize it, feel it, and release it to God. There is no better feeling in the world than to be in control of the pain that once kept me cemented from living my life.

I practice the saying "this too shall pass" if you say it often enough, you will have complete control of your pain in a way that is empowering. I choose to take my power back and honor my emotions, and know that they are there because I choose them to be there.

I am learning to steer clear of making rash decisions when I am in this state of pain and loss. I am especially learning to listen more to the inner me and heal her first before appeasing others. I have learned to think before I speak truly; sometimes, being silent is all the healing you need.

I still ask for signs from above, and when I am still enough and am in a place of pure trust in God, my signs appear. I smile and say a little thank you for the reassurance. We are all connected to God within. One day that little flame within you will burn brighter than it does today.

Although I am not a mother, I recognize the relationship that I left was a toxic one and not one that would be good for any child to be a part of. Maybe that's why God never allowed it to be; however, I know that God is real, and his plan for me is real, and that mustard seed is ever-growing.

Is the pain still there today? Yes…yes, it is, only now I can push past it with gentleness and love for the inner mother in me.

Anna Pereira is a successful Real Estate Agent in the Greater Toronto Area since 2011. Anna settled in the GTA in 1990, where she furthered her education at Sheridan College, George Brown College, University of Waterloo, and the Ontario Real Estate Association.

With a soft spot for helping others, Anna became an accredited counselor for Abused Women and Children in Ontario in 1997. Since that time, she has been a volunteer in Social Service settings and finds helping others fulfilling and humbling. Her career and interests have taken her down paths of executive business roles to now a Top Producer in Real Estate.

She continues her volunteer work with her Church as a Choir member and continues her dedication through volunteering in the community. Anna enjoys music, singing, writing, and all things real estate.

Contact: email: listwithanna@gmail.com

Facebook: https://facebook.com/annapereiraipro
Instagram: https://www.instagram.com/annapereirarealtor
Twitter: @Anna Pereira Realtor
Linkedin: https://www.linkedin.com/in/anna-pereira-realtor-2844a211/

10.

THE LOVERMORE MASTERPIECE

Lovemore Sher McLaughlin

It is a beautiful sunny day here in Ajax, and the rest of the household is enjoying the pool and the outdoor.

As I sit in my Lovemore lab preparing to share, I greet you in love and today's Overflowing of Appreciation. I give thanks for the opportunity to see and share the message from the messy pieces of my story. My wonderful friend Debra had asked me to write a chapter of 2500 words. So, here I am with a winning visualization, celebrating and giving thanks in advance for being a part of this bestseller Pursued by purpose. I am already on my third listen of one of my favorite songs, Refinery by Maverick City. In deep reflection, I realized the most significant chapters of my Life's story (outside of the birth of my angel Sade in 2006) are from 2010 to 2020. This decade is a combination of my most painful experiences, the catalyst to self-awareness, acceptance, and my biggest transformations to date.

2010
2010 was one of the lowest times of my life. As I type, I recall not combing my hair for about six to eight months. I remember wearing a hat to hide the proof that internally I was crying. One of my most embarrassing moments was

a site inspection visit at a corporate location in Pickering. I had to do a Christmas catering delivery and wanted to do a site run-through to ensure the day of delivery went smooth. I had to go through security with my client, and in the dreaded moment, I had to remove my hat.

Can you imagine under my cute catering attire was a sign of brokenness, despair, and loss? I am such a professional, and it goes to show our outer appearance; the suit and tie imagery are not always an indication of the truth of our heart and soul. My heart kept nudging things were not going well, but I did not fully understand what it meant to listen from within. I was longing for more but was not sure what I really needed. My self-worth was exceptionally low, and as a chef at that time, my lack of self-value affected my brand and personal life. The constant circle of low self-esteem and self-knowing kept me feeling low inside.

My life at this time consisted of work and more work. I was not getting enough sleep; I would speak to close family members on the phone in a hurry. I was always on the go with my mind consumed on getting an order complete, plotting out staff needs, designing catering displays in my head, and sometimes barely being present in the moments outside of my work task.

Another not-so-proud moment was one day I was getting ready for an event, my brother called. Mom handed me the phone, and I spoke fast, like running and out of breath. I lack being present in the moment. My mom gently shared how I was always rushing on the phone and daily living and bad. I felt bad and wanted to do better but never understood the power of being intentional, making choices, and taking actions I kept wishing in my head.

As I pay attention to how much of my time was spent toiling, I realized I had to create a feeling of home at work. So I gifted myself a tabletop sign that said the Purpose of Life is a Life of Purpose. I had seen the message on display at a local UPS store, and I knew right then I wanted it for my catering signage tabletop display. God was speaking to my heart back then; right at this moment, I smile as I glance at these beautiful, meaningful words. A great reminder to make each day meaningful with purpose living day by day.

2015
February 2015, I took mom to Sunnybrook Hospital filled with hope and lots of faith amidst her cancer journey to get her next set of updates and results from her myriad of tests. As the doctor gave the results, I thought I was asleep and having a bad dream. She said mom only had three months. Mom was so far gone mentally and emotionally she did not fully understand the news. I still hoped in my heart a miracle would happen. Each day Mom's graduation seems to be just as the doctor had predicted. Instead, mom slipped and shrunk into another dimension each passing day. This is a journey I wish on no one. I have witnessed firsthand life being diminished each second right in from of my eyes.

During these moments, for the first time in my life, my mom's last name (Lovemore) had a new significance in my heart. I felt horrible not celebrating this beautiful legacy for 43 years. One day as I supported my back on the wall in the hallway, I found myself on the floor, uttering, "omg, this journey is a message for me. Oh Lord, you are speaking to me". I do not have the right words to explain, and I know that I know in my heart that Mom was passing on her customized legacy and life purpose over to me. Mom never chose her legacy, and most people do not. It is so custom for us to identify the legacy of someone when they have graduated and sometimes do not celebrate them when alive. The main thing I did during this painful experience was to make a choice. I realized I could choose to live the rest of my life honoring the Lovemore legacy.

This beautiful legacy Mom carried in her name for over 60 years. Mama Lovemore graduated to heaven in April 2015. Her Graduation opened my eyes to life. Before she left for heaven, she made me promise to find my own happiness. She could see that I was barely existing, and her words illuminated that I needed a change. Losing my mom was the catalyst that opened my eyes to how lost I was. I slowly started the choice to heal and found true joy in the Lord. In July 2015, I also gave my heart to the Lord and got baptized at mom's church. This was the start of my healing and the journey to more self-awareness. In July, I also moved and came to live with my aunt. My eyes slowly started to see the abundance in each day, from the sky to the chirping birds in warmer months to tracing the luxury of my breath, especially in the mornings.

Lovemore started to shape me; I was becoming more beautiful, overflowing from within. Around 2016 most of my new social media contacts started to call me the Love lady, Lovemore lady. I got up each day committed to learning how to love myself more and appreciate the beauty in each moment and day. Each year after 2016, I learned more about who I am, the places I loved, the seasons that I loved the most. I started to see the beautiful colors in fall. Autumn is my favorite season. I must say that I have grown to appreciate the snow.

On my self-discovery, I have grown to love the outdoors, especially the lake. I come most alive at the lake; the closer I get to the water, my mind and heart feel peaceful. If I have a low day, I run to the lake. Around 2017 I started to wear vibrant clothing and jewelry. My top colors are yellow, orange, fuchsia. Vibrant, energy, happy, Joy, smile are the words that are always used when describing me. I was learning to Lovemore. I was doing so much better; it was noticed by so many, I was happy, thankful, and living more. My self-care was so much better than before, I was noticeably happy, joyful, and learning to be present. I extended and shared my Joy daily, and my internal transformation was evident. Most of the areas in my life I worked on consistently but……….

2020
In December 2019, I was reflecting on How I wanted to move forward. I wanted to be known as an example of daily love and as Lovemore. So, on January 01, 2020, I changed my social media name to honor my parents. Lovemore Sher Mclaughlin, Lovemore honoring Mom, Sher Short version for Sherine and Mclaughlin to honor my dad living in Jamaica.

Personally, I was growing, continued to soar in self-love, choosing to live more, and had a heightened appreciation for everything.

Within the five years, I made lots and lots of wonderful internal changes. However, there was one area in my life that needed to change. I was still working too many hours.

I honestly wanted better in this regard, but I felt I could not take the time to stop as I was concerned about how I would pay my bills. As a result, I was only getting around two hours of sleep most nights.

It was Friday, February 28, and I arrived in Niagara Falls for a lady's retreat. It was a bitterly cold day; I had arrived early to unload and get ready for the ladies, way before they arrive. As I pulled in to park, my van got stuck in a puddle. I unloaded and focused on the weekend. I was so excited to connect with the small group of ladies. I clearly realized the best part of the event was connecting, hugging, and serving these ladies through Joy in all the experiences from food and all in between. Overnight it got colder, and in the morning, my van was frozen in. Nevertheless, I enjoyed the weekend and made some heartfelt connections. Sunday, I packed and headed back to Ajax, went home to grab some items, and headed straight to the kitchen.

I got to the kitchen before my team member, and I was beyond exhausted. I had only gotten a couple of hours of sleep in Niagara Falls. We had a few setbacks in the kitchen, and I sent my team member home to get some sleep, and I stayed overnight. I went home to shower and grab my chef's jacket and a few other items in the morning. I went back to the kitchen, and in a state of exhaustion, I broke down crying; the ugly get me a large box of Kleenex, wailing cry. I was tired of being tired. I cried, "Lord, please help me do better." I have had it; I honestly did not want to go to the event. My team member had to drive me, and I prayed all the way to my event silently in my heart. Finally, we met up with my other team members. The event was an awards ceremony at a University in Toronto. My team members had never even seen me this way; my eyes were red and teary.

After unloading, I pulled myself together; I had a show to lead and execute; from table designs, art pieces are woven into floral presentations, I had to present my signature experiences that thousands have loved over the years. Once I started creating and designing, I felt better; it was light, camera, action. The event was a huge success. My team members drove me home, but I was not feeling well. Again, the crying started before I hit the bed; this time, it was, Oh Lord, I am tired of being tired, and 18 years of no vacation has taken a toll. Lord, I could use some rest. I could use a vacation.

Our first Covid lockdown was a week or so after.
After a week of adjusting to the news of Covid, I realized this was my vacation wrapped much differently than I had envisioned. I decided to accept this was God's way to me personally to rest. I gave thanks this season for my time to rest. I had time to listen to God. I had time to walk daily and clear my mind. I had time to go to the lake at least once per week.

I reconnected with a beautiful memory of attending a family fun day with mom at my Primary School. I had entered a dance contest and won. So I started to dance sometimes for 2 hours per day, I would also connect with my online community, and we danced virtually together. I was experiencing life on a whole other level. I was getting eight hours of sleep per day. I finally got the time to look into the eyes of my household. I got the time to hug my daughter when I wanted and if I wanted.

In June, I realized it was time to create a plan, the lifestyle I wanted for myself and my daughter. The first thing I did was create a Lovemore Masterpiece vision board. At the top of this plan was 8 hours of sleep per day. In addition, this plan included creating GPS toolkits that would allow me to practice daily self-care habits. One of this GPS was a God-powered system. God would be my daily anchor, this vision board was also a dream of mine, a Lovemore Lifestyle prayer and gratitude Journal. I am delighted to announce the Journal was launched in December 2020.

After praying for my next direction, my team member sent me a Life coaching course link. For many years other coaches and a few friends kept encouraging me to become a speaker and a Life coach. But, to be honest, I have fought to become a coach since 2015.

As I seek the Lord for my next direction and reflect on all that I went through, I asked myself what I will do with the lessons I have learned. I knew my heart is committed to Lovemore. One of my frequent prayers is, Lord, when others see me, let them see you. I was afforded time to love me more, and I relied daily On God for his daily guidance. Each new day I was addicted to inspiring others to Lovemore. Even more than ever, with lockdown and everything online, more love is needed, and I was ready to love myself more and show others the Joy from the process.

With my increased Joy and daily self-care, I wanted this for others, especially fellow businesswomen. Businesswomen who are burnt out and feel like me but cannot stop due to financial reasons. So, in September

2020, I registered Lovemore Lifestyle Inc, with three pillars. One of these is Lovemore Life Coaching.

I have realized on my journey so far that Purpose is living each day honoring God and loving ourselves and others. So I am definitely living in my Customized purpose.

A few days ago, my daughter put her head on my chest and asked for us to sing her favorite song. "The more we are together, Together, Together, the happier we shall be. My heart desires to see us as brothers and sisters of the world live daily in love, our unique gifts, and our customized purpose, blessing others with our uniqueness. We are each being pursued by purpose in our own unique way. The Purpose of Life is truly a life of purpose and Love.

Lovemore Sher Mclaughlin decided to change her name in January 2020, on all Social Media platforms and for her speaking engagements to Lovemore.

She has committed to honoring both her parents by celebrating their names. Lovemore spends her days learning to be a true vessel Of God and his love. She emboldens and inspires us to manifests the best in each of us through love and appreciation.

Lovemore resides with her angel Sade and a huge household of family.

Lovemore is by profession an inspirational Chef, Lovemore Life coach, and creator of the Lovemore prayer and gratitude journal.

Contact: blessings@lovemorelifestyle.ca

https://www.instagram.com/lovemorelifestylecoaching/

https://www.facebook.com/sherine.allison.16

11.

A PATH TO VICTORY

Nicole Waldron

What happens when you feel that something is pursuing you and you are not sure what it is? Do you run, do you wait to see, or look back, or do you stand in anticipation with excitement?

Being pursued by your purpose can stir up some of, if not all, these emotions.
I have been pursued by purpose from a young age. For me, Purpose is what we do on the way to fulfilling our Destiny. Recognizing that the purpose of what you are doing will change in time. Yet, we are all created with a Purpose on purpose by the One who has a purpose for our lives. As we embrace what life offers through this earthly journey, we learn and grow more along the walk.

When you walk in the fullness of who you are—being purposeful—you will have a new joy and freedom to be you and live in your authentic self. In the past, I have been down on myself trying to figure out my purpose, yet it was when I paused and allowed myself to be and speak to the right people in my life (**my Iron Sharpeners**) that I got back on track. **Note**: Your Iron Sharpeners must be of the same element, **"Iron,"** with the capacity to build you up and keep you sharp.

I focused on doing the things I loved and not focused on the money. Truth be told, there are times I wish I focused more on the finances, but I would say I was oblivious to certain things. Honestly, this has brought some regret as I am not where I would like to be financial. However, if I were to put things into perspective, my heart was happy. I had set a vision for my family's emotional health above all else. In addition, I was doing things that I loved and contributed to the community. Now that is ***priceless.***

Let's be real; when your purpose pursues you, it is not always a smooth road; however, you must keep in mind the vision. Think about this: the way to get to the most beautiful waterfalls can be a rocky one. I think of being in the islands, going up narrow and winding roads to get to the best waterfalls. However, to experience the most spectacular views, you must go up high, above sea level. There is nothing more spectacular.

Sometimes the journey to get there may take you up some winding roads with many twists and turns, and you may not see what is in front of you; you may not even see what is behind you. What you do know is that you are headed to a particular place with a significant view. What propels you forward is the **Vision.** This is key to you walking purposefully.

I had a lot of knowledge and information; however, I did not fully understand, which hindered me from walking in the wisdom I needed for some of the seasons in which I found myself. You see, I needed to know and ensure that I understood to walk in wisdom towards fulfilling my purpose. But, the beautiful thing is that God is merciful, and His Grace is sufficient. As a result, I was brought to a new place of humility, as I reflect and see that when I was lost and had some missteps, God was ready to redirect me and to catch me when I fell.

The more I reflect, I see when He brought opportunities in the crisis and used my experiences to propel me forward. No matter what happened, I realize my purpose was, and always has, pursued me. Even in what I thought was a mistake or even a failure, these experiences provided me with what I needed for my journey. It fortified me in a whole new way.

Honestly, there were times I let that loud voice, that imposter, the accuser, the liar, overpower the truth that can at times arrive through the still small voice that will set you free. The lies believed took root and took me off the path, but God, who is faithful, again brought me back on track. He ensured I had some key individuals in my life who would speak life into me, even when I was not, even when that imposter was speaking to me. The funny thing is that there were times I would turn on the TV or watch something on the internet, and there would be a similar theme, whether it was addressing my fear, my doubts, and uncertainties, along with the confirmation that I was going back on the right path.

Life can be so funny at times; I really believe in six degrees of separation. I connect with people now who I met a long time ago but did not even recall meeting them, and the moment has become a full circle, one in alignment with my purpose. There are even those times when I had some really challenging experiences in a job or with a relationship, and little did I know that it was preparing me for now. Even down to the books—confession, I am a bookaholic.

I recall watching a show and seeing Dr. Caroline Leaf, a neuroscientist, who was making great breakthroughs with the correlations of the brain to mental health. I bought her books and listened to her avidly. Then, one day a friend asked me to host a talk show, and we combined it with a conference – I told her about Dr. Leaf, and she got her to speak at the conference.

So here I was on stage about to introduce a woman whom I had admired for years. What a moment that was! Even more so when she personally spoke into my life, I was blown away. Now today, I see her on even greater stages speaking to the world. Now I am operating in mental health spaces, and I am again using her teachings with greater insight and tools for projects I am working on. This is just one example of when your purpose is pursuing you – it's the great connector moments.

Don't ignore any situation in life. This is one of the things I know for sure. Things will eventually line up and make sense, even when you are not paying attention. The bigger reward comes when you pay attention and realize all the crooked places are being made straight. God will direct your path; even when you may enter those places that are dark, He will lead you to the light. My life is a testimony of this. Interestingly, we prefer to believe the negative or the lies when the accuser comes at us rather than listen to the beautiful voice of truth. We need to stay in the light of truth, and it is the only thing that will negate the lies.

As I wrote this, I reflected more, and I saw how things

have lined up. I did have a vision for my life, and my intentions were family-focused in one area; however, I left out certain areas. Therefore, I can now see that it must be for every area of our lives when creating our vision boards. I must acknowledge how many times fear stepped in after unexpected situations that blew my confidence and threw me off-kilter in areas I did not even see. I was living in a bubble, but I did not know it. As a result, I stopped taking risks in certain areas of my life, though I was brave enough to advocate for others yet not for myself. But God, whose grace is sufficient, has been kind and gentle with me; he advocated for me when I could not do it for myself.

It is true: delay is not necessarily denial. I am reconnecting the dots, I have gone back to the blueprint, and I am adjusting where necessary. Same canvas, same paint, different application. The good news is, the vision was always there; I could see it in my notebooks, the things I did, and the people with whom I surrounded myself. You see, when your purpose is pursuing you, there will be clues along the way showing you what to do. It will show up in many areas of your life. You must recognize the signs and know that there is a process as you walk towards the fulfillment of your destiny.

I recognized that to do this; I would need a new perspective which led me to create a new mindset: a **V.I.C.T.O.R.Y** Mindset. As I use this for myself, I also coach others on the Victory Formula: **Living a Victorious Lifestyle, a Life of Purpose.**

Victory and Vision
Create and recognize the value of vision. Vision is vital to living a victorious life of purpose on your way to destiny.

Therefore, we need to create a vision for every area of our lives, starting with self (mind, body, soul, and spirit), family, health, partner, career, and finances.

You must really envision it, not just write it down—make it plain. Take the time to invest in this because it will give you a blueprint for your life, and your purpose will start to evolve. Our vision is unique to us—it's God's fingerprint upon our life. We must yearly review our vision, for as life changes, we at times need to adjust. **Living a victorious lifestyle starts with the vision.**

Inspiration and Intention

Our vision requires inspiration, be inspired by your vision—this will provide the much-needed fuel for your purpose. Our intention is necessary for a successful implementation of our vision. It helps bring clarity and set the path to achieving the goal.

We must ask ourselves if our intentions are "me" centered or "we" centered. What's inspiring you? *Living a victorious lifestyle requires intention and inspiration, being intuitive, looking at what's inside you, paying attention to that still small voice within.*

Cultivation and Creation

Creativity is needed as you cultivate the vision. What are the seeds you are carrying and want to plant? What type of fruit do you want to be in your life? What do you need to nurture your vision, and how will this help you pursue your purpose? Cultivate your vision like you would the most beautiful plant in your garden.

Before you plant a seed, you prepare the soil; then, you nurture it while it goes through the process of death, which will eventually bring new life. First, the **seed must die to self**. Metamorphosis happens underground in the dark as the seed transforms; the ground around it needs to be cultivated to thrive. **Living a victorious lifestyle includes cultivation—prepare the soil, kill the weeds, nurture the seeds planted. Cultivate it—be creative, understand, and know what those seeds are for.**

Transformation through Trials

The transformation will come in stages and the various areas of your life. It will transport you into many experiences, and some may even look like dead places or failures. In the transformation process, we need to be tactical—I refer to the seeds. The seedling now starts to come above ground from the dark and must deal with new elements as it grows—there are various seasons in nature, including various temperatures and elements.

The process is a time of change to which the seedling must embrace of its own to become a full-grown plant or before it can flower and bear fruit. Before it can produce it can be part of the circle of life and give back, the plant had to develop to another stage of hardiness.
Living a victorious lifestyle brings transformation—your mind is renewed; you make choices and decisions that lead you to victory.

Ovation and Orchestration

There must be a celebration through the various processes of change—sit back and recognize your growth.

Some growth changes may be small and hard; others who are not going through it will not see it. Now you know it because you experience the stretching, and sometimes you feel stronger or weaker depending on the day.

Like the seed, you need to know that there is something

greater outside of the darkness because, through the storms, there are glimpses of the light. The seed must ensure that its roots are deeply embedded in the soil to withstand the various elements. This is where external help is needed.

It would help if you had the Iron Sharpeners. They must be qualified to be in your life, willing to foster your growth, ensure you have the positive things around you, and celebrate your small and big victories. They will help you find perspective and remain objective as you thrive.
Living a victorious lifestyle requires an ovation, praise in the middle of it all. It's an orchestration—bring the orchestra pieces in your life together and create the melodies of synchronization; it will be the strength to your bones.

Restoration and Redemption

Restoration can be like a process of redemption—where you must be robust. This happens in the time of maturity—as the plant is about to come into its fullness—to operate in that for which it was destined to grow. First, it had to go through the seasons, and now it's ready to be in full bloom.

The fruit is getting ready to come forth after its flower formation; then, it experiences another redemptive process before turning into the fruit. It has withstood the elements and the seasons of change. It understands what to expect in some areas, yet it's getting ready for new ones. This is where purpose has been realized. Despite the challenges of different seasons, it now understands why it was created.

The seed matured into its fullness and is utilized. If you do not know what seed you are planting, it will not be developed or used well. Unfortunately, there are times in our lives where we have planted ourselves in the wrong soil and must be replanted after a period of growth and in the right season so that we can be restored to that for which we were created.

Living a victorious lifestyle ensures restoration and replenishment in the power of purpose. Once you stay in the process, you will arrive at places of redemption.

Yield and Yearning

The path to victory includes yielding to learning, and you must

be humble, teachable, and as your purpose pursues, you will end up operating in victory. Before you move along the path of purpose, look from the end to the beginning— and your purpose will be made clearer, and you will prevail. **Living a victorious lifestyle includes yielding to the process as much as you are yearning for the desired outcome. Trust the process you're in, lean in, and surrender.**

V.I.C.T.O.R.Y.

V- To reignite the **visions** that we carry.

I- To **inspire** each of us to walk boldly in our lives purpose.

C- To **cultivate** the dreams inside of us.

T- To remind us to embrace the moments and times of **transformation** even when there are trials.

O- To **orchestrate** our celebrations – it's ok to celebrate who we are and others in our lives- we are not here to compete against each other but to complement each other, thereby becoming our best selves and helping others along the way.

R– To r**eplenish** and **restore** hope in hearts, to those who may be feeling little or none, as hope is necessary for our hearts.

Y- To say yes to ourselves and navigate the process of **yielding** so we can **Live a Victorious Lifestyle.**

A professional event specialist, an inspirational speaker, thought leader, community advocate, voice animator host, author, and podcaster, the multi-faceted Nicole Waldron works tirelessly for the advancement, progress, and prosperity of her community. She serves on various boards and committees, working to advance her community and advocate on several issues.

Nicole is the Brian Burch Community Service Award recipient, the Outstanding Community Service Award, and the SHSC Kathleen Blinkhorn Award for Excellence in Volunteerism. In addition, she was named one of 150 Women in Canada by How She Hustles' HERstory in Black and one of the 100 Accomplished Black Canadian Women by 100 ABC.
Contact: nyohance@yahoo.com

https://www.facebook.com/nicole.d.waldron

https://www.instagram.com/victoryspeaks7/

12.

COMING TO CANADA

Blessing Ajayi

My name is Evangelist Reverend Mrs. Blessing Ajayi. I am excited to share the Joy, experiences, challenges, and lessons I have learned on my coming to Canada from Nigeria over sixteen years ago. It has been a dream Journey of purpose and the values earned are worth the sacrifices. I thank God for his sufficient grace to carry on.

Beloved, thank you for taking the time to read my chapter. I really appreciate your presence. May I remind you that God loves you? Always be thankful to him. It is not by chance that you are reading this chapter right now, but God planned it for you by divine appointment. So kindly pay attention and read to the end. I am very sure that it will be blessed.

Everything in life will cost you something. Every decision you make in life has a cost, and it is applied to every area of life. I feel blessed to have come to Canada, especially with my family. A place where God unveiled my vision. A flourishing land for my treasure and possession. A chosen nation for my generational inheritance and greener pasture. Canada is my promised Land.

Jeremiah 29:11 AMP, *"I know the thoughts and plans that I have for you, says the Lord, thoughts, and plans for welfare and peace and not for evil, to give you hope in your outcome."* God knows your outcome. Seek him, and he will guide your path."

When I migrated to Canada with my husband and our three children, I was pregnant with our fourth child. I was a businesswoman with purpose, industrious, virtuous, and spiritually grounded in faith. My husband worked in the oil and gas industry. We were doing very well as a young couple. Nevertheless, we chose to leave everything we had behind and relocate to Canada to give our children dual citizenship opportunities, good education, and hope for the expected future.

Growing up as a teenager living in Nigeria, my sister had invited me to visit the United States of America three times; each of the application processes, I was denied the visa at the interview, indicating that I may not return to Nigeria. In my disappointment, I had courage; then I told myself that the next time I would travel abroad will be with my family, and we will surely make it.

I got married to my husband and realized he had had the same experience traveling abroad; Nevertheless, we believed that God would make it possible and beautiful at his proposed time because what God cannot do does not exist.

Proverb. 16:3 AMP, *"Commit your works to the LORD, submit and trust them to him, and your plans will succeed if you respond to his will and guidance."*

However, I had a revelation about my Canaan Land, and The Lord spoke to me that my family and I would go to our

Canaan Land, a place filled with milk and honey where I will fulfill my purpose and destiny. I remembered for a few years I was praying about it, and I decided to leave it in God's hands. So when the opportunity came, we embraced it knowing his words had come to pass. The evidence came sooner than expected, and we were approved permanent resident visas to migrate to Canada.

Following all the trials and challenges that we went through, the Holy Spirit revealed that we must get ready to leave for Canada immediately. Stating that our unborn baby should be delivered in Canada. It was made known that my country was not safe for us anymore. My husband was concerned about the short time for preparation. It is usually difficult to get a ticket for a woman over 7 months pregnant, so I insisted prayerfully, we booked our tickets.

The Cost Of Purpose For Your Destiny

During one of my prayer sessions, I was instructed to financially support a God-fearing pastor with my house and store, which had 2 years of fully paid rent. Ordinarily, we would have rented our house and sold the store to gather money for our trip to Canada. I prayed, and I told my beloved husband about it, and he accepted.

The giving continued; I sent to another man of God to benefit from my blessings. I gathered all the money that I saved in USD; I went to a Church and gave it to a man of God, he was surprised. On the day I handed over the money to the chosen Vessel, I was crying because it was a sacrifice of obedience, and I told him it is what God instructed me to do, he blessed me, and I left. Little did I know that the battle had just begun. A few days later, I was hospitalized for a few days; I was eight months pregnant, the Doctor recommended bed rest for me, and he advised that I minimize any pressure and stress.

My little boy fell ill a week before our journey to Canada. The severity of his sickness could have stopped our journey, which was what the enemy planned. During this incident, I told my husband that we must leave. My boy was extremely sick and lifeless, and I was praying that God would grant us victory. We decided to leap of faith by leaving Nigeria with my sick son. I only had three weeks until my delivery date, and I was not having the baby in Nigeria because my life was in danger and that of my son.

I remember when we were escorted to the airport, he was in critical condition; it was a life-or-death situation, but I was strong and prayerfully courageous, trusting in God's promises that if He said it, then I believe he will do it. I knew that his blessings for our life journey would make us rich and add no sorrows. My son will not die but live to proclaim the goodness of God. I was praying and crying that God would not put me to shame, and to God alone, I sing a new song and dance my new dance.

We got to Lagos, and my son was lifeless for days; he was treated with all kinds of medication. Yet, my faith was strong, trusting in God. I cried, reminding him of his covenant promises with me for my life and my family. Our journey was like the Israelites on their way to the promised land where it looks like crossing over was impossible; regardless, we had faith and kept believing that God can do it because he is not a man that he should lie to me.

He is a God who keeps his promises, a great healer. I

kept meditating on his word that he is too faithful to fail me and never will he put me to shame. Indeed,

God put my faith to the test, but I refused to be moved by the situation. Counting my blessings, I remembered that God had saved my life during the delivery of my sick son. I confessed that if God Almighty did it, then He will do it again now.

My husband said to me, "why not stop this journey in Lagos and plan it for another time." I then said to him, "what God has started, he alone will complete, and no power can stop it." We have gone too far to give up now; he did not start with us to leave us halfway; we will continue to wait, worship, and praise him. I prayed all through that night, asking God for grace and improvements on my son's health so we can head to Canada. The following day, we bundled him by faith, and we left for the airport to Canada.

AMP." *A man's mind plans his way [as he journeys through life], But the Lord directs his steps and establishes them."* Proverbs 16: 9

Coming to Canada was a journey ordained by God. I remember I made a covenant with him that if he saves my son and removes the shame and reproach on my Family and me, I will serve him forever, praise him and proclaim his words. I will dedicate my son and service to him. God gave my son strength and kept him alive throughout the flight until we landed in Canada. Immediately as we landed at the airport. My son was rushed to the hospital, and he was admitted for a few days. It was surprising to know that the healthcare system paid off all the bills we incurred, and by his grace, my son became well again and was discharged.

I delivered a bouncing baby boy, our last child. We named him Emanual (God is with us) and Olufemi (God love Me); God saw us through the battles and gave us victory. He saved our lives and added another precious gift to my family. My husband and I were incredibly grateful that it all ended in praise.

May God continue to bless the pastor and his wife and the entire members of RCCG Kings Court Brampton, a loving and caring family church. At the time of the naming ceremony, I was a novice. I did not know what to do because of the stress I was going through. But the church organized and sponsored the naming ceremony of my son. I was surprised and grateful.

New immigrants are encouraged to see the church as a place of shelter and shield. Find a Church family; they will always love and support you as you go through integrating into the Canadian system of your new life.

When we came to Canada, my children stayed with a relative with a family of six: him, his wife, and four children. Likewise, my family had four children. We were all doing fine and happy. One evening, the children were all playing and making noise, their mother called for bedtime, and one child continued to play; the mother became angry and smacked him. The following morning, he went to school, and the teacher asked him about the mark he had on his shoulder; he said he was smacked with a belt and the teacher reported to the school aid for investigation.

The police came and picked up all the kids to their custody for days while they went through the legal matter. This was a horrible experience for my family and me. We were sad about the incident. Imagine seeing your children being taken away, though they were alive but not home with you. I prayed fervently for their release and to God be the glory; the court decision was in their favor.

The family went through an emotional crisis and reconciliation process at this season of their marriage. My children and I became extremely uncomfortable shortly after the children returned home. This is an experience I wish I had avoided. If I knew what I know today, I would not have agreed to share with another big family. I was nursing a newborn baby, and it was not safe and healthy for both families even though we are related.

My sister, who came from the United States of America, saw the pressure I was going through to take care of the children alone, especially our newborn baby. She applied for a US visa to join her in the state, and we were denied. Immediately She got us a three-bedroom basement apartment and furnished it. The children's rooms were decorated with Disney characters of their choice. It was a happy day for us.

When we came to Canada, people were not readily available to spend time with newcomers because of their busy schedules. Every new immigrant to Canada needs a helping hand, someone who can contribute financial support and time for them to integrate emotionally and mentally into the system. The support my sister rendered to us in our situation was a saving grace. Oh God, bless my beloved sister, Caroline Egbelu. She will live a healthy long life to enjoy her children and great-grandchildren.

We moved into our new home after three months of staying with the family. This was one of the best transitions we made, having freedom in our own little space where we can decide what we like and how we chose to do it without any feeling of offending anyone. My sister stayed with us for two weeks and taught me many things I needed to know; where to go shopping for the kids, how to make my choice of food, how to educationally engage my children, be my children's chef, took them to the library, used the library resources, played at the park, engage them in recreational activities and more.

She took me through the "new immigrant school of knowledge and thought." Two weeks later, she went back to the states. I remember that night we were awake discussing everything she taught me. My sister groomed me so well within the short period of time she spent with us in Canada; she did what I had not gotten from anyone. She had a great impact on me. I was empowered and ready to reciprocate my love and kindness of gratitude with those women and families going through their immigrant transition process.

She equipped, empowered, mentored me spiritually, physically, and emotionally to settle, be happy, and live independently. She reminded me of the strong, virtuous woman I was in my country before I came, and she encouraged me to do it again and make it through with our four little children alone until my husband finally joins us in Canada. Then, when she was leaving for the airport, we both cried so much, but I assured her that we would be fine, and I will do my best to take good care of the children with God's help.

During this time, I built up strong courage and self-esteem. I started improving myself and my children. I bought a double stroller for my two youngest to make it easier to move around. I engaged them in recreational activities, swimming, Ballet dances. I was involved and committed to church activities; I hardly missed church services. Fortunately, the church protocol picked us up and dropped us for Sunday and Wednesday services.

I felt at home, being a part of a loving church family. I met a few families who care a lot about us. On weekends they would invite us for dinner, some bought groceries, bring their fine, used clothes for my children, and many other good things. I was loved and cherished.

I became aware of the busy work system here because people do not have time on weekdays, and the challenge of work and bill payments was a top priority. I also had a good friend with four children who lived in an apartment. She invited my family over to spend the weekend with them at their place. As a newcomer to Canada, I discovered that I had to push myself to engage socially and communicate with people, even asking for help when I needed it.

I was appointed to teach the children's department in my church, and I started to engage more with the parents of the children. In communicating with the parents, I realized the majority were refugees and new immigrants; once I began to tell them my story and how good it will be to get their children to engage and perform in church activities, this brought them closer to me. Eventually, I noticed that most of the women migrated here with their families, but their husbands later return to resume work in their country, where they made a living to support their families. So this was how my humanitarian service ministry started in Canada.

AMP: Romans 9:17. *"For this very purpose, I have raised you, that I might show my power in you, and that my name might be proclaimed in all the earth."*

The experience of my season of integrating into the Canadian system helped me see the struggles, challenges, and necessities from the inside. It was too transparent to ignore them, especially from my point of view. I was willing and passionate to help those who needed my support. Everywhere I went, I met women who were depressed, lonely, and isolated, especially in the church where people came to worship God, seek protection and solutions to their problems.

I started to devote my service to new immigrant women and families in the church. I called them and followed up with them after hearing their story. I also encouraged, prayed with them, and focused on helping them to meet their basic needs. This stage of transition is essential. I literally applied the unconditional love my big sister shared with me when transitioning into Canadian lifestyles.

The Word of Knowledge and Inspiration For Purpose

I will make you a great nation; I will bless you abundantly and make your name great, exalted, distinguished you. And you shall be a blessing, a source of great good to others. I will bless, do good and benefit those who bless you. And I will curse the one who despises and dishonors you. And in you, all the families (nations) of the earth will be blessed." Genesis 12:2-3

I Will Not Give to God Anything That Costs Me Nothing

In pursuit of purpose, I passionately go the extra mile to reach people in need. I once operated a grocery store that was a center for my Charitable services. Refugees and new immigrant families would shop in my store and go away with free food. Having this level of impact made me happy and felt accomplished. This obedient act of sacrifice through prayer, compassionate care, and humanitarian service birthed the vision of my Ministry.

I often organized food and clothing campaigns and distributed donations to shelters and food banks. I also travel to African Nations to conduct conferences, open-air crusades, community outreach in orphanage homes, seniors' homes, Prison and correction centers, widows, and people with disability challenges. The faithfulness and mercies of God have humbled me in various areas of life and Ministry. I have come to realize that God deserves the entirety of me and that of my family.

Commitment, devotion, worship, and praise; to him alone be all the glory. For this reason, I declared that I would not give to God anything that will cost me anything. In pursuing my purpose, I had given up myself for the service to God and humanity. I gave up my businesses, Career, commitments, resources, friends, time, and leisure in good faith. Yet, these can never pay the price for his unconditional love and sacrifices to humanity. God desires our voices to praise, worship, and proclaim the good news of the gospel of salvation. The Great news is that each of the costs comes with redemptive benefits that create a deep fulfillment on a level that will bring you to your knees.

The pursuit of purpose enabled me to invest and achieve the things I am passionate about. It is the road map to the fulfillment of my destiny. God gifted me with multiple purposes; I find my purpose when serving in the place of my calling, doing the things I love to do according to God's gift to me. It has helped to find meaning and value in every work of my life. My passions are targeted in evangelizing the gospel of Christ, sharing the love, and transforming power of God, service to humanity, Outreach to support the less privileged and people in need, helping people to discover their potential and purpose. Community development and program to empower the youths, women, seniors, marriages, and families.

My experience from the challenges I faced when we came to Canada led me to my vision. I was able to use the impact to help humanity and new immigrant families. My encouragement, coaching, and support to the vulnerable made a difference in our community. My joy today is that regardless of the battles that surround us, my dream came to reality. By his grace, I am living a purposeful life. However, my husband and children are blessed, and We are happy together as one big family.

Rev. Blessing Uwuma Ajayi is the Founder and Chief Executive Director of Glorious Women of Wonders Worldwide, a registered charitable organization in Canada and Africa.

She is a philanthropist, a woman's voice advocate, and a humanitarian ambassador who has consistently served and supported the vulnerable population on a national and international level for more than Fifteen years. Her goal is to demonstrate God's love to humanity with an unwavering focus to do charitable works, helping underprivileged, oppressed, and unreached people.

Rev. Blessing is an exceptional leader, a virtuous woman, counselor, mentor, missionary, and evangelist who has traveled around the globe to conduct evangelistic revival Crusades and meetings such in Africa, Nigeria, Ghana, Tanzania, where she mobilized her women outreach ministry over ten years. Her compassion and act of goodwill for humanitarian purposes have changed many lives.

She is the mother of her four biological children and has been married to Mr. Abayomi Ajayi for twenty-three years. She lives in Brampton, Ontario, together with her family.

Contact: blessing.ajayi@yahoo.com

https://www.facebook.com/gwomenofwonders

http://wvgc.gloriouswomenofwonders.org/

13.

JOY COMES IN THE MORNING

Debra Wright

> *For his anger endured but a moment; in his favor is life: weeping may endure for a night, but joy cometh in the morning.*
> Psalms 30:5

Have you ever cried through the night, waiting for morning to come? I am sure many of us have been there at some point in our lives.

As a young girl growing up, it was always my desire to be a mother, and since I was the eldest of seven children, I was like a mother to some of my younger siblings, and I was delighted to help my mother with the younger children. Then, as I grew older and got married, I felt that it was finally my turn to have my babies.

I was twenty-one when I got married, and at the end of that year, I began to get the signs of early pregnancy. We confirmed that I was indeed pregnant, and I was ecstatic. Unfortunately, as the months went by, I became extremely ill and found myself hospitalized almost every week. I was diagnosed with a condition called hyperemesis, which is constantly vomiting. I would become dehydrated and had to be given an anti-nausea medication intravenously. I hated this, but if this was what I needed to do, I just had to do it.

As I laid on the hospital bed many days, I cried and asked, "why me?" All I wanted was my baby, my friends were all having children with seemingly no problems, and here I was so ill. When this was happening, I was just wrapped up in my own sadness, not because I could not have a child, but because it was not going as I had hoped. I was despondent and frustrated. *Even when things do not go the way you want or plan, still trust the process; it is important.*

The months rolled by, and I started working part-time because I wanted to feel normal and enjoy the pregnancy. In my fifth month, I started experiencing some unease and was a little bit concerned. I did my monthly check-up, and everything looked fine, according to the doctor.

One day as I was on my way home from work, someone hit me in the stomach at the train station, I am not sure if it was an accident, but I began to cramp and bleed. I ended up at the hospital, and for three days, I was in agony. Finally, on June fourth, nineteen-eighty-nine, I gave birth to a beautiful daughter who lived for a few short minutes. Nothing was wrong with her, but she was just twenty weeks and could not live. My husband and I held her as we mourned our loss.

I cannot tell you the emotions that I experienced that day. I cried for a while, and for a long time, I thought of her every day. A few months later, I discovered that I was again expecting. This time I was careful about where I went and made sure I was doing everything I needed to do. I again began to experience hyperemesis and was again in and out of the hospital. I could not keep anything down in my stomach. I prayed that God would help me to feel well.

At sixteen weeks, I felt a sharp pain in my abdomen, and when I went to the washroom, I was bleeding and had to be rushed to the emergency room. There my baby was trying to make an entrance into the world. I cried and prayed, and for a little while, he stayed put. That night the doctors recognized the condition causing me to miscarry my babies; it is called an incompetent cervix. The doctor tried a procedure called Shirodkar suture, and right after coming out of the surgical room, my water broke. My heart sank! He lived for a few days and died in utero, unbeknownst to the medical staff.

I was released from the hospital because they told me my baby was still alive with a good heartbeat. I honestly do not know what happened there because I developed a high fever after getting home one night. I was rushed to the hospital in pain and was very scared, not knowing what was happening. My life was in danger because I became septic.

Having parents that prayed was what kept me alive. As my parents entered my hospital room, my father said he sensed a dark presence of death in the room and began praying. I was hemorrhaging because the baby was already deceased and decaying; I was not delivering all the debris from the placenta or the fetus. When I finally delivered the baby, I did not even know what happened to me. I knew my son was gone, but everything else was a blur.

Before leaving the hospital, the doctors warned me not

to become pregnant for at least six months, but in my heart, I just longed to have a child, and in three months, I was indeed pregnant again. I hid my pregnancy from my family until nausea started, and I was in and out of the hospital.

I knew my family was distraught because of what I was going through, and I just wanted them to be happy for us. They were, but because of what had transpired previously, they were cautious about being excited. This was understandable. At ten weeks, I started bleeding. My cry was, "Lord, how do I handle this now"? I cannot lose another child. My heart hurt as I still had thoughts of my precious babies. I longed to feel them in my arms, so I just kept praying and crying out to God.

One morning, my girlfriend, who was also pregnant, took me for a second opinion; the doctor I saw told me to abort my baby; we were so angry that I did not even know what to do. My girlfriend's family doctor was a few minutes away from the Obstetrician that I saw, and we decided that I should see him as well. As we got into the office, a sense of peace came over me.

This doctor was an elderly gentleman, and as we began to speak, I told him of my experiences and what I was now going through. I will never forget the words he said to me. He said, "My dear, children are a gift from God, and if it is His will to give you the gift of a child, no one can take that away from you."

The tears were streaming down my cheeks as I left his office. The day before this meeting, I had done an ultrasound and was told that the placenta had a tear, so I was worried. That evening after we left the doctor's office, we had a midweek church service. I had to use the bathroom, but I really needed to get out because I felt overwhelmed about my condition. A sister at the church walked in and saw me crying; we spoke for a little while, then we began to pray. I told the Lord that I could not bear to lose another child and if he would please help me.

The next morning, I had a follow-up with my obstetrician and an ultrasound. This is where we began to see the work of the God I serve. Whilst at the ultrasound, the technician, kept looking and checking. I was so curious to find out what was happening at the time because they are not at liberty to give you any results. I had to wait until I got upstairs to see my physician. I went upstairs to the doctor's office, and what he said was interesting to me. He told me the tear was not there anymore.

Wow! I said to myself, God had just healed me, he heard my prayer, and now my baby was saved. I was able to have a Shirodkar suture procedure at my twelfth week and carry my baby. This pregnancy was not without its ups and downs. Lots of hospitalization, but the pregnancy was progressing. I was finally going to have my baby.

We found out that it would be a baby girl at the six-month mark, and we were ecstatic. God blessed us in the new year with a beautiful baby girl by cesarean section. She was perfect and beautiful. Everything I had asked God for, she was, all that and more. My family rejoiced at what the Lord had done. As I sat on my hospital bed on that snowy morning with my arms finally full, I looked down at my beautiful daughter; I checked her fingers, toes, and every inch of her body. She was perfect! I was rejoicing at the goodness of God.

Sometimes as I sat back in reflection, I could remember my empty arms and heart. I did not know what would happen to me in my quest to be a mother, but God did not forget me; he had heard my cries and prayers.

Six months after my beautiful daughter was born, I fainted, and I remember my mother-in-law asking me what was wrong? Honestly, I had no idea what the problem was. I went to the doctor and explained what had happened and that I was not feeling well. He asked me if I could be pregnant? What? "No doctor, I said, my daughter is still breastfeeding." You see, I was under the false impression that I could not become pregnant because I was breastfeeding. I got the test, and the next morning it was confirmed. Oh, Lord! Now I was really getting my arms filled. My son was born prematurely, but he was a big and healthy child. When I got pregnant with my second child, the doctor advised me to have a tubal ligation, but when he was born prematurely, I was advised against it. Sixteen months after, God blessed us with a third child, another son. My third miracle baby!

My quiver was now full, and after what I had been through to have them, I was quite happy to be done with making babies. Four Shirodkar procedures, three cesarean sections, and the months spent in and out of the hospital were worth every pain I felt and tear that I cried. I now had my children, my gifts from God.

Psalms 127: 3 "Children are a heritage of Lord; they are a reward from him.

As my children grew up, we encountered many blessings and many trials, but I always gave God praise for them.

They were sickly for a while, which wasn't easy; despite that, I was thankful to have them. During their teenaged years and high school, as most parents go through, I had challenges with them; they were taught the principles of Christ and brought up to be respectful and to serve God.

There were some amazing achievements and some disappointments, but I genuinely enjoyed being a mother. Life became difficult financially, and our family was broken as they entered their early twenties, but they stayed close to each other and me. I love them with all my heart. As our lives changed, I found out I was going to be a grandmother. I had thought about this but did not think it would be this soon in our life. I was happy to know that our family was growing, and I would meet the next generation.

The day my grandson was born was another surreal day for me. As he was placed in my arms that day at the hospital, I cried again because I realized that this child was an extension of me; he was my sons' son. It was a great moment for our family. This child came in the darkest of times for us; he was like a light in the darkness we were going through.

We loved him and loved on him but did not spoil him. I thanked his mom so much for bringing him into the world. Five and a half years later, we had another addition, a little girl, and then another little girl from my other son; soon, I know we would add more grandchildren to our family. It was then that I realized why I could have never given up on the desires of my heart. To be a mother was my heart's desire; sometimes, I wonder if having them was a greater joy than the marriage itself.

I cannot tell you the feeling of having my family around me, enjoying the love and joy they have given me.

I have had the privilege to meet many women experiencing some of the same things that I had encountered in my life. There is a kinship and sisterhood when talking about the issues we faced with losing a child or children. When you have walked the road they are now walking or have gone through; you can empathize with them. It says that you really do not know what she feels until you have walked in her shoes. My heart is to help a sister who is walking that road. I may not be able to carry her the whole way, but I can hold her hands and dry her tears.

Had I given up hope, my journey would have been quite different. Instead, the hours in tears, pain, hospital, and prayers allowed me to cherish my children even more. As I look at them today, each one is so different but so alike in many ways. People often told me I had a rainbow, as all my children were different in color, my daughter pale in complexion, which prompted a nurse to doubt me when she asked me if my husband was white. When my husband came in, she just shook her head.

My second child was slightly darker with beautiful big brown eyes, but my last baby was a very dark little boy with thick curly hair. Why am I sharing this? God beautifully and wonderfully made each child from my garden, and today as I look at them, they love each other and make sure they are there for each other.

From this journey, you can see the hurt, anguish, and pain that I had to endure was rough, but this journey was priceless to be where I am today from where I now stand. Through the storms and the pain, God kept me. I was able to achieve what my heart desired, to be a mother. Would I change it? Maybe just the part where I lost my daughter and my son, but even in that, I still say, "Thank you, Lord!"

Weeping may have endured for the night, but Joy came in the morning.

Debra M. Wright is Forgiveness Life Coach, Motivational Speaker, and a Bestselling Author.

Debra is an affiliate with Americas' #1 Confidence Coach Dr. Keith Johnson and the Destiny Coaching group.

As a forgiveness life coach, she has had many situations in her life that have set her on this journey. Her passion is to help women that have gone through broken relationships, by separation or divorce, to get to a place of freedom from resentment, anger, and bitterness. Debra will take you on the forgiveness journey and help you to let go so you can live a better life.

Debra is the host of her show Real Talk Forgiveness on the Speakup and Empower Network and Host of Kingdom Authors Forum on the Virtuous Entertainment TV Network (VETVN)

She is an award-winning Leadership and Speaker with Christopher Leadership Lumen Association.

Contact: debra@debramwright.com

https://www.instagram.com/debramwright1/

https://www.facebook.com/Debrawright21/

Website: https://www.debramwright.com/

14.

I'M A BIG GIRL NOW

Cheryl Moses

At four years old, I felt like such a big girl. I was in primary school now. I had my chalk and slate to write on, and I was excited to learn. Everything I learned, I tried my best to teach my younger sister, who was two years old at the time.

It was lunchtime, and I was finally home from school. I still had my school uniform on, but my hair and clothes were disheveled as usual. I did not understand when I was told…. quite often: "Make sure you come back looking just how I sent you!'" That was a mystery to me. The most important thing to me currently is that I was home, and it was lunchtime.

Most days, I would excitedly give my little sister a play-by-play account of the entire school day. My elder siblings usually helped prepare the meals amidst laughter and whispered tones about teenage things, which I would later understand.

I still have a vivid memory of my mother sitting quietly in a rocking chair by the living room window, away from the fanfare/festivities in the kitchen with a solemn look on her face. My last memory of my mother alive was in the dismal hospital ward, with an IV bag hanging and a plastic tube from the IV attached to her hand. Our new baby brother was lying in a basket beside her bed. The room was so quiet as my elder sister and a couple of us younger ones stood there looking concerned at our mother.

My mother died later that night. She left us a few days after giving birth to her twelfth child. My mother died at forty years old, leaving behind all of us….and that was that. The flurry of activities that ensued her departure was incredible. First, I cannot remember anyone explaining to me what was happening. I remember my father holding his head, collapsing in front of the house, crying uncontrollably. My older siblings were all crying, and lots of people from our village were coming and going as they brought food and more food; they talked and sang late into the night. My little sister, brother, and I played but with an unsettling feeling that "something big" was happening, but we did not fully understand what it was. The grief of my family and our extended church family was great. My dad was well known. He was a loved pastor and a very personable postman for many years.

Seeing my mother in the glass coffin going down to the church in our backyard was surreal. I wondered to myself: "Who is that person behind the glass?" That day I realized that my mother died. "I am a big girl now, and I could do everything for myself" was my new mantra.

What happens to a young family after a mother dies? How do you repair the space left in the hearts of her children? Where does the widowed grieving spouse get the strength and clarity to navigate the direction and wellbeing of his children and his life? "Tough times don't last, but tough people do!" I remember a scripture that has given me strength: "For I know the plans I have for you declares the Lord, plans to prosper you and not to harm you, plans to give you hope and a future." Jeremiah 29:11. Proverbs 19:21: "Many plans are in a man's heart, but the purpose of the Lord will prevail." God opened a way for my father and his children to immigrate to Canada, and he also provided another mother for us.

My mantra, "I'm a big girl now, and I can do everything for myself," was put to the test. The next few years in my homeland were a whirlwind. My sisters, who were all young adults, took turns caring for their youngest siblings as best as they could. I lived with family friends, but these times were short-lived as I was considered "sexy" by older occupants. I did not want to be sexy. Fortunately, I did not fall apart. God had something greater for my life. This scenario happened on several occasions as a young child. One day, I decided to write a letter to my father in Canada telling him about my demise. I showed the letter to my grandmother, and she promptly took the three youngest children in and watched over us like a "hawk." We have moved around to different households several more times before moving to Canada.

I still remember when we got the news that my little sister and I would be traveling to Canada. We promptly said goodbye to our friends and family as we excitedly awaited the day. Neither of us had ever been on a plane before. When the day came for us to travel, we laughed and cried because we were so nervous. We hugged our grandmother, who we would not see again. Soon after we left for Canada, she also left the island and traveled to the United Kingdom, where her son and family lived; she died a few years later. A gallery was covered by glass in those days where some of our relatives stood and waved at us as we walked on the tarmac towards the plane.

When we arrived in Canada, they told us to put on our sweaters to walk outside of the terminal building because it was November, and winter was in progress. We shivered as we walked towards the building, and when we got to our first escalator ride, we froze and stared at each other. We had no idea how to jump on. Looking back at that experience, I always smile. After living in Canada for so many years, an escalator mount and dismount is not a big deal. My father and my siblings, who already moved to Toronto, were so happy to see us as we were to see them, but we were timid and whispered to each other for the first couple of days.

I was in awe when I experienced my first snowfall. It was so beautiful. Long icicles were hanging from the trees and wires. We learned to make snowballs and crafted our first snowman with a carrot nose. Back then, I thought the whole wintery scene was amazing, but now I am delighted at only the first snowfall, and that is about it. I would rather see it on television. We learned to skate that first winter and really adjusted to living in Canada quickly. We only had a few dark-skinned children in our school, but I did not feel out of place. Being a minority in many settings was normal to me as this became a repetitive pattern throughout my schooling and employment.

A lot of children in my classroom were so intrigued with my accent. They kept saying to me: "could you say that again." I smile now, thinking about those times. We discovered that NHL hockey was so exciting. The Stanley

Cup Finals grabbed our attention, and we were slowly learning the Canadian ways. We learned to ride the subway lines and follow the maps. At twelve years old, I took my first streetcar ride to meet my older sister downtown at Yonge Street. She was only 16 at the time. We went shopping at Simpsons and Eaton's and then went out to a steakhouse for lunch. Those were extraordinary memories. She always bought a Calderone chocolate bar for me. Our sisterhood bonding started to become cemented from then. You see, it is not always the big things that matter. It was important to her to spend time and give me a special treat occasionally. Relationships!! Life is meaningful because of the relationships that we nurture.

I had times during my teenage years where I questioned my self-worth. I never doubted my ability to understand intellectual things, but I questioned if I looked good enough for someone to fall "head over heels" in love with me (this is from reading all those Harlequin romance novels). I was not as selective in choosing my boyfriends. Fortunately, there were no major disasters......I am still in one piece. High school was full of sports and music, and new experiences. I loved it.

At 16 years old, I joined the Canadian Army reserves. I became a Corporal in a Communications Regiment in Toronto. This is where I met my lifelong friend, who also joined with the promise from the recruiters to "travel the world." The furthest place we traveled to was New Brunswick. I think they conned us......just saying. The military helped me to develop mental toughness. I remember one of our field exercises where we had to provide sentry duty and make sure the enemy did not overrun our camp. All I remember is being cold, tired, and feeling sorry for myself as the mosquitos played a buzzing symphony by my ears and bit me in every exposed crevice they could find. But I signed up for that.

"Independent": that was me. I was always trying to do the things that interested me. I did not need someone else to validate my area of interest. I did very well in school and aspired to become a "mad scientist," Later in my teenage years, I considered becoming a marriage counselor. Funny enough, I did not do either of these things. After high school, computer programming was "hot," with lots of opportunities opening for graduates. So I thought, why not? Off to George Brown College, I went and graduated with a Business Administration Diploma, but I soon realized that I absolutely could not sit still for so many hours.

I reasoned that I would be fired for falling asleep at the desk. God designed things so well. My sister, who treated me to lunch dates when I was younger, was in her final clinical year at Toronto Western Hospital in Respiratory Therapy. I asked her if I could come and see what she did. She took me around the hospital to see the patients that she cared for. I was not scared at all. I was totally fascinated by the patients on ventilators and the equipment. I cannot even remember the hospital smelling funny. I was certain that Respiratory Therapy was right up my alley. It fulfilled two criteria:
1. You can move around the hospital.
2. You can talk to people. I did not know exactly what was required of the job, but it satisfied my criteria.

I have never regretted my decision. Health care is my

passion. I love caring for others and encouraging them not to give up on themselves. I have trained and functioned as an Acupuncturist and natural health "pundit" for many years, learning as much as my poor brain would allow. However, something in me goes into driving mode when someone is in physical pain. It is the strangest thing. I must resist the temptation to sit them down and knead out their achy joints. I have a fond memory of one of my favorite ICU doctors, sitting down in a stupor at the nursing station after one of my massage and acupuncture treatments. His tie was untied and off to the side of his neck, and he had a dreamy smile on his face. After he announced that he had a headache and that his shoulders hurt, I went to work on his aches and pain with a smile. He did not know what hit him. I literally could not help myself.

I have been blessed to sit with patients and hold their hands praying softly as they slipped away into eternity. Sometimes their family was not able to make it to the hospital in time. The paycheque is nice but being able to make a difference for another human being is priceless. A patient recently gave me the greatest compliment, and I felt an immense sense of gratitude along with a sense of satisfaction. She said: "Thank you so much for being with me through my procedure in the Emergency Department. You were like an angel to me."

The last few months as a Respiratory Therapist in the acute care hospitals has been a bit nightmarish in the scope of what we experienced as health care workers and the acuity of our patients. The one thing that I was able to do the most was to help patients in my care reduce their fear and stress levels. The next thing I've done many times over is the pep talk: "If you want to get out of here, you have to fight this. Do not take this sickness lying down. Fight!! Do not give up!! I often prayed inside: "Lord, come on the scene."

As an emerging young woman, the life concept that I learned in high school and college during the 1970s and early 1980s was to be a self-sufficient woman. I grew to believe that I did not need to depend on any man to take care of me. I could take care of myself. I passed this on to my girls and many younger ones. Is this good advice? Maybe. Maybe not. To my eldest son, I preached: "women like a good-looking man, but if you have nothing to give them, they are going to go with the bald head, big belly one." In other words: "talk and good looks are cheap; you have to be able to deliver the goods."

I have had many disappointments in my life, but I truly believe that my successes have outweighed any defeats I could have faced. I have loved and lost but never allowed myself to give up. God has blessed me with a God-fearing, family-loving husband, four amazing children, and three "super smart" engaging grandchildren.

What would my next chapter hold? I am excited to find out. I am destined to receive all that God has ordained for my life. Why did I hang on during the dark days? Where did the drive come from to keep pushing... to work, learn, achieve, and encourage others to go for their dreams and not give up? I have been asked on many occasions: "Where do you get the energy to do all these things?" I usually smile and say to myself that I have a stubborn will; that is all. Now I can answer: "I am pursued by the purpose that God has ordained for my life."

How about you?

Cheryl Jackman Moses was born in the isles of Trinidad and Tobago.

She immigrated to Canada at the tender age of 10 and is now considered a Trini-Canadian. She is a born-again Christian.

She is married and has four children and three grandchildren. Cheryl has been a Respiratory Therapist for most of her adult life. She loves health care so much that she has studied, trained, and practiced Acupuncture, Chinese massage, and other natural therapies.

Caring for and encouraging others is what Cheryl does best.

Contact: cmoses19@finmail.com

https://www.facebook.com/cheryl.moses.752

15.

AGAINST ALL ODDS

Carlton H Wright

For the first nine years of my life, I was like most boys my age, curious, playful, and inquisitive. Catching insects, fish, lizards, and sometimes, the occasional birds. Playing in our neighborhood streets and yards was the norm. We would play cards, marbles, softball, house, church, and so on. When playing church, I would often play the preacher. My favorite bible stories were the stories about "Moses and the children of Israel," "Joseph with his coat of many colors," "Joshua and the walls of Jericho," "Samson and Delilah," and "David and Goliath."

Most Sundays, my older brother and I would attend Sunday school. It was a traditional church in Spanish Town, Saint Catherine. We would frequent mister Rodney's candy store to buy candies or chewing gum on our way to church, making sure not to spend our offering. Sometimes we would walk through the cemetery or across the train tracks. The area was beautiful, bushy, quiet, and play heaven for two young boys.

It all started when I was approximately ten years old. First came the fevers, later diagnosed as rheumatic fever, then the inflamed joints and joint pains. My wrists and knees were often stiff, swollen, and achy. Eventually, the doctor discovered a heart murmur, but there were no other symptoms or issues. Within six to twelve months, my condition got worst, and I was eventually admitted to the hospital. That was the beginning of my health struggles.

I did not sleep well for the first few nights that I was admitted to the hospital, but I eventually adjusted to the new setting. The doctors, nurses, and staff did their best to make me feel comfortable and at home. The food in the Spanish Town Hospital was commendable, but there was nothing like my mother's prepared meals. It did not take long for me to start missing the family table.

After a few days, my mother or my father would bring my meals whenever possible. I looked forward to whatever they would bring for me each week. Oftentimes I would forego the Hospital's food for my mother's cooking. The rice and peas, and chicken or the curried goat, etc., were the highlights of my weekend dinners those days. Some days I would eat late at night after my visitors were gone because it was comforting to me when I was alone. You would not know it now, but I always had a passion for mother's food. Thanks, mom!

The grounds of the hospital had many shrubs and trees. So many birds were living in them; robins, red-breasted thrust, grass quits, mockingbirds, or nightingales. Every morning was like a gift to me. The sights and sounds of a new day were always welcoming. Regardless of how I felt, the early morning sun, and choir of birds, was always uplifting. I had a special liking for the mockingbirds, and their song always seemed to be the sweetest and most musical. Being ill had heightened my senses and appreciation for the world. Nothing was taken for granted.

Despite all the pains in my body, I took time to reflect and enjoy the world's beauty around me.

During my admittance to the Spanish Town hospital, I saw many cases of burned and poisoned patients. It was hard for me to see so many cases of children who suffered these atrocities; accidental ingestion of bleach and other household cleaners, falling into fire pits, or some other types of burns. I often wondered why so many adults, primarily parents, were so careless with their children. I know accidents do happen, but it just seemed that there were too many. It was painful for me to see those cases almost daily, feeling their pains but not comforting them. Most of these incidents were allegedly accidents, but I often wondered.

The nights were sometimes long and lonely, but I would often find comfort in reading the bible. Whenever I felt alone and or afraid, I would read Psalms 27:1. *The Lord is my light and my salvation; whom shall I fear? The Lord is the strength of my life; of whom shall I be afraid?* Or Psalms 23:04 *Yea, though I walk through the valley of the shadow of death, I will fear no evil: for thou art with me; thy rod and thy staff they comfort me.*, and whenever I needed the encouragement of my faith or strength for my sick body my healing scripture was,

Isaiah 53:4-5, *4. Surely, he hath borne our griefs and carried our sorrows: yet we did esteem him stricken, smitten of God, and afflicted.*

> 5. *But he was wounded for our transgressions; he was bruised for our iniquities: the chastisement of our peace was upon him, and with his stripes, we are healed.*

I do not remember how many times I was admitted to the hospital, but I became a regular patient. After my discharge, I had many outpatient visits, and I regularly went for checkups and medications.

After our mother migrated to Canada to be with our father, my siblings and I went to live with our grandmother in a little town outside of High Gate in the parish of St. Mary, Jamaica. There would be no more convenience of running water; we would now be fetching water from our community spring or the standpipe. There was also a river nearby in which we would sometimes fish and take a bath in the river. There were no more streetlights but starlight; however, it was nice to hear the chirping cricket and singing toads at night; they became our nightly lullabies.

It did not take long for us to adjust to living in the countryside; we made friends quickly and within a few weeks became a part of the community. One day while going to school, I noticed that I could not keep up with the group; the incline was steep, and I ran out of breath, huffing and puffing. That is when I knew that things were changing. It was not a good feeling being left behind, no longer able to run with the pack. The things that I took for granted a few days ago were now a challenge. Once I was healthy and strong, now I was feeling sick and weak.

Adjusting to the changes in my body was physically and mentally challenging; it was a difficult thing to do. Breathing was now a laborious task. After a while, the changes in my demeanor had become so noticeable that the children gave me a nickname. It was not one that I approved, but I was too weak to fight it, so it stuck.

Eventually, I was admitted to the Port Maria Hospital in St. Mary. Again, the doctors did the best they could, and then I was discharged. Again, I became an outpatient, this time at the Highgate clinic in St. Mary. I did not know that the doctors had given up on me. They had done all they could, and the rest was up to me and my faith in God. I was grateful for the prayers of the saints, my parents, strangers, loved ones, and friends, who never gave up on my deliverance. The amazing thing was that I never gave up on myself though many people gave up on me.

We were overly excited to migrate to Canada, as we had not seen our parents in years. Arriving at the Pearson International Airport was a beautiful experience. The lights on the runway from the air, and the city, were a beautiful sight and most welcoming. We were excited to see our parents, and the new addition to our family, our baby sister.

We arrived in Canada in September, and adjusting to the sudden change in climate was another traumatic experience for me and my siblings. I think out of all my siblings; I had the most difficulties adjusting to the new environment. The end of the Canadian summer was a serious shock to my tropically cultured body, and it did not take long for me to start missing the chirping crickets, singing toads, and the outdoor showers of Jamaica. I had an adjustment crisis. It was difficult for me, and it took some time to get accustomed to the cloudy, wet, bone-chilling cold of the fall season.

As fall turned to winter, getting to see the snow up close and personal for the first time was a delight. The freshly fallen snow was clean, white, and pretty, and as the winter season progressed, we learned to make snow angels and snowmen.

Six months after arriving in Canada, I was scheduled for my open-heart surgery at the Sick Children's Hospital in Toronto to repair a leaky heart valve. Before my operation, I pledged to dedicate my life to the Lord, which was the beginning of my Christian journey.

The surgery was successful, and I had floods of emotions going through my mind. I felt like a piece of myself was missing, and I was crying without any understanding or explanation. Then, finally, I remembered one of the nurses asking me why I was crying, but I was happy and sad at the same time. I think the reality of what had happened to me had finally hit home. It was an emotional time for me. It was probably a combination of the morphine plus the sense that my body had changed, and I would never be the same again.

After my surgery, I was given a wheelchair to get around the house and go outside not to exert too much stress on my heart. As a result, I was restricted from walking and climbing the stairs. This was my mobility device for the next few months; therefore, I spent most of my time on the first level of our house. At nights, when it was time for bed, my father would help me up the stairs to my bedroom.

During my convalescence, I started playing the guitar because the music helped fill the void, heal my spirit, and soothe my emotional pain. After I was healed enough, I started playing the guitar in church. I loved to play the songs of Zion, songs about the Jordan River, Lion of Judah, and the uplifting choruses.

While at church one day, I guessed one of the sisters noticed my struggles after the usual meet and greet; she said to me, "the devil is going to make you feel pain, but he is a liar, don't believe him." For many years, those words would be my pain medicine. Every time my joints would hurt, those words would soothe me like a balm. Her words encouraged and taught me how to have faith in God regardless of how I felt mentally or physically.

Being sick for so many years made a permanent impression on my young life. I was broken, broken in body, and broken in spirit, but I had learned to cope through it all. I have learned to always look on the bright side of things; the sun is always shining behind those clouds. While there is life, there is hope. So do not let the negative memories keep you down.

What is in your past cannot harm you anymore. The pain is only a memory; don't let it trigger you into that endless cycle of reliving the painful past over and over, and over again; do not give it power over you or your relationships. Don't let the painful memories hinder you from having meaningful or intimate relationships with family or friends. Unfortunately, so many people's lives are controlled by negative experiences; they avoid intimate or meaningful relationships because of the fear of being hurt or betrayed. Don't project your negative experiences into your impending future. It is a memory that is now under your control, under your power. You are the only one that can break the trend.

I trust that this story touched your heart; know that despite everything, you will be ok. I have seen God work in my life, and I am happier because my health is better now. It can be the same for you. God is a healer, and no matter what health challenges you are facing, God can do the same for you. God bless you!

Carlton Wright was born in Jamaica and migrated to Canada. He is by profession a transit worker with one of the cities transit corporations. He is married to his wife, Debra, and together, they have six adult children and grandchildren.

Carlton studied music at Berkley College of Music in Boston, Massachusetts, and has played guitar for many groups, churches, choirs, and bands. He is a defender of the faith.

Contact: Email address upbeatcarlton@yahoo.ca

https://www.instagram.com/carltonwri/

https://www.facebook.com/upbeatcarlton

16.

NO DRAMA

Ruth Dente

Walking out of the hospital feeling relief but still thinking, would I make the same decision again!

It is amazing how God does things that we can look at it and say, this must be the hand of God. Growing up with two older sisters and four brothers was always lots of fun. When my sisters' friends came over to our house, there was always lots of girl talk, "fairy tale" stories about life expectations, planning, and daydreaming. One such story that would pop up was how many children they would like. Of course, everyone would have their own number and their extravagant reasons for desiring to have either seven children, like our family or three or just one.

That part of their conversation was always entertaining, but as they grew older and had talked about the birthing process, I would quickly slip away. I was never interested in hearing the stories about how many hours some people took to bring forth a child. There were one too many stories of 28-hour contractions and dramatized stories of the water breaking on the way to the hospital and hours and hours of pain. It just was not my cup of tea to listen to what I thought were, for the most part, negative stories that I felt would not be my reality.

Years later, I found myself having my first child. As we went to our doctor's visit when they received the results of our first ultrasound, it did not reveal the gender of the child. The Gynecologist quickly told me that it was better to have a healthy child than redo the ultrasound to determine the gender. We agreed and never asked again. Sometime during the pregnancy, the Lord spoke to me concerning my unborn child, so I told my husband we would have a girl, and her name will be Charity.

My daughter Charity was two weeks overdue. One afternoon as we did our regular Doctor's visit, he checked me and found that my baby was not in a position to come as I was not yet dilated. The Doctor said, "If you are not dilated a few centimeters by the next morning, then you would have the child by Caesarian "C-section." He booked us into the hospital for seven-thirty the next morning. That cold wintry night of January 20, we made sure that we packed our bags into the car and everything was ready. We went into prayer, and this time, God gave me a scripture; it was Psalm 121. Indeed, our help comes from the Lord, the one who is also the creator of us all. God is exact. Our appointment was less than 12 hours, and I had no contractions. Of course, we would prefer to have a natural birth, and we knew that God would have to intervene.

As I laid there in the hospital that cold January morning, we received the news that God had done it, my cervix was dilated. They induced me, and now it was a matter of time before the pain began. According to an article, "Induced labor can be more painful than natural labor. Women have told me specifically that the synthetic form of oxytocin causes stronger, longer, and more frequent uterine contractions than natural contractions."

Yes, God had already come through many times, but my next hurdle was that pain was not my friend. I had never been here before, and so as I lay and looked down at my stomach, fear took hold of me. No one knew the terror that was flooding my mind. I was petrified. Subconsciously, it was etched in my mind that my grandmother died during childbirth. As I laid there in silent terror, I had to self-talk. I began telling myself that there were many people in this world and so many millions of people who have given birth before so that I will be fine. I reminded myself that God had a plan for my life and the baby, and we would make it out safely. Fear is torment. I began to meditate on the word of God, the scripture that he released to me the night before. *"The Lord shall preserve thy going out and thy coming in from this time forth, and even forevermore."* (Psalm 121:8 KJV)

As the contractions came, to my surprise, they felt like menstrual cramps. Either I had terrible menstrual cramps, or the birthing process and pain were a breeze for me. Perhaps the pain would have increased, but I did not wait to find out. My doctor had prescribed the epidural for me, and that is what I had. It certainly was not the drama that I had overheard by everyone quick to share their dramatic and sometimes theatrical but true stories. Of course, as I mentioned before, I avoided these stories. Deep within me, I always believed that my story would be different.

It was no coincidence that my daughter Charity was born that afternoon of January twenty-first. Ironically, or as God would have it, my first-born child was born the exact number of years and days to me as I am to my mom. I later learned that my mother was also induced with me. I did not come willingly.

The hospital was full of many visitors, including a couple of people who saw an angel of the Lord right in the room that evening. There is an incomprehensible peace when God shows up and has a purpose in our lives.

I was about three months pregnant with our second child, and the unthinkable happened. One day, while at work, I received a call from the doctor's office asking me to come for a visit right away. As I left my office, all the way home, I was in tears, and my mind was racing for fear of the unknown.

As we sat down with the Doctor, she told us that our unborn child had an abnormal test result and that her recommendation is to have an abortion. Wow! What? This is serious and totally unexpected. After she explains probable outcomes, we told our doctor that we are Christians and that we will have our baby by Faith. The Doctor, as precious as can be, wrote on our chart, "they are Christians, and they are going to continue this pregnancy by Faith." It is so important to have faith.

The next day, as I returned to my office and spoke with one of my colleagues, she told me that her friends went through similar situations of negative test results during pregnancy. She said that some of her friends went through with the abortion, and some bore their children and their children were healthy and fine. Her knowledge on this topic was a real comfort to me. God always has a witness to encourage us in the time that we need it the most. *He is our very present help in times of trouble.* I do not remember worrying about my baby, as I left the outcome in God's hands. I knew that he had been there for me before with my firstborn and that he will come through again.

As our firstborn, our second baby was also overdue, and so I had to be induced. I told the nurse straight away that I am not good with pain that I need some medication. She told me that I should inform her as soon as I needed it.

Occasionally the nurse would enter the room and find me laughing and as happy as can be. She would look at the monitors. Finally, she said to me, "I thought you said that you were not good with pain? Let me know when you need the epidural." God did another miracle; He caused me to not have any labor pain, even without medication. However, I was scared that I might cause harm to my child when giving birth, and so from not having any pain, I had pain in my neck and shoulder from getting into a fetal position and staying as still as possible for the epidural process. God was doing something new, but I did not understand it.

When our little daughter Faith finally arrived, she was perfectly normal, healthy, and as happy as can be. God is a miracle-working God. When we trust Him, He always works things out for our good. But, unfortunately, fear sometimes tries to get into the driver's seat and causes us to make decisions that we could wind up totally regretting. Living and trusting God takes faith, but it is worth it. HE always comes through.

Children are such blessings. They view their parents as heroes. I have learned that, to a child, their dad is the biggest, strongest person in the whole world, and their mom is the most beautiful, kind, and loving person. So we certainly have a great responsibility in nurturing our children and providing the best environment for their spiritual, physical, and emotional growth.

Having my third child was another testimony of the Grace of God. As I lay in the hospital room after being induced, the nurse came in to check on me and was amazed that I was smiling and pain-free, unmedicated going through contractions. It was only about three hours of being induced, and my baby was ready to come. Finally, the nurse walked into the room, looked at the monitor, and then looked at me and said, "This here is perfection."

There I was lying on the bed, looking around, chatting, and laughing and my monitor showed that I was having contractions, no medication, and no pain. God did it again! He gave me the grace to bear my child without the pain of giving birth. This time, I did not take any medication and went through gracefully. I remembered that awful feeling and the pain that I experienced in my neck when I cowered in fear, and God gave me the courage to go through this time in total faith. At last! No epidural and still no pain. We did it! I trusted God.

Watch lives align to the things that we have spoken about. I had said and always believed that my situation would be different. I did not take on anyone else's story as mine. Yet, here I was, at home the next day with my third child, and I had just birthed my third miracle.

Interestingly, I was induced with my three girls. They were so comfortable in the womb that they did not come out on their own. So it was a no-drama situation. Everyone's life is different. We all have a different story.

The above testimonies are what I shared with a young lady one day as we walked in the mall, we got on the topic of childbearing, and so she told me that although she and her husband were married for seven years and had been together for ten years, they were not able to conceive. It just was not happening for them. I felt compassion towards her as her parents, who lived overseas, constantly asked her for an update on their anticipated grandchild, but there was nothing to report.

I know what a joy it is to have children and how God had blessed me with my miracles. I began to speak into her life, and I asked her if she was ever prayed for about their situation, and she said, "No one prayed for them." I asked her if she would like me to pray for her. She quickly said yes. We sat in the mall during our lunch hour as I laid my hands on her and said a quick and simple prayer. I then gave her some important instructions. Faith is an action. Buying a baby's crib, diapers, or clothing after reciting a prayer, is a step of faith. She began to walk in faith.

About five months later, she said, 'I can't wait to see you. I have great news. I am pregnant. My husband and I are having our first child.' God had done it. What an amazing testimony of the power of God. They are raising their beautiful miracle baby girl to be a mighty woman of God.

In life, do not despise the hard kernels; everybody loves a fresh bag of popcorn. Things may sometimes look tough, but it forms into what God ordained it to be with a little time. I am reminded of Joseph as he faced countless trials, and there came a time in his life when he said, *"But don't be upset, and don't be angry with yourselves for selling me to this place. It was God who sent me here ahead of you to preserve your lives."* (Genesis 45:5, NLT) He recognized that God was his Shepherd and was guiding him the whole time.

If Joseph focused on the prison walls or the lies they told him, he would have given up on his dream. There would be a different story. Despite the many roadblocks he faced to experience the promises of God fulfilled in his life; Joseph pursued purpose. He did not stop; he kept pushing through. God was with Joseph. God is us. God takes our pain and exchanges it for purpose. We are encouraged to *"count it all joy when you fall into various trials, **knowing** that the testing of your faith produces patience. But let patience have its perfect work, that you may be perfect and complete, lacking nothing."* (James 1:2-4, NKJV)

Until the time that his word came: the word of the Lord tried him (Joseph). (Psalm 105: 19) When we face tests and trials, it is for a season and a reason and a testimony in the making. In the end, there is testimony that will be a blessing and encouragement to those who hear. The bible says, *"And they overcame and conquered him because of the blood of the Lamb and because of the word of their testimony"* (Revelation 12:11, AMP)

Being pursued by purpose is not an easy process.
It may get ugly sometimes.
It may feel pain sometimes.
It may feel like an eternity.
But in the end, it shall show forth the strong will of God for our lives.
There is light at the end of the trial.

For a great and effective door has opened to me, and there are many adversaries. (1Corinthians 16:9, NKJV) Great purpose comes with great challenges. When there is pressure on an orange, the juice comes out plentifully, and we enjoy it. We are refreshed by it.

The Lord was with Joseph and caused everything he did to succeed. Therefore, whatever you put in God's hands, he will take care of it, and he will cause it to increase greatly.

We go through things, and we grow through them. Things that use to cause us to be overwhelmed, we grew past it. We learn from the things that we go through. We also gain wisdom, knowledge, and understanding that we can help others.

When we share our testimony, I have learned that it becomes someone's source of victory, strength, and encouragement that they too will be okay. Most of us have an experience of how we felt unfairly treated, lied on, falsely accused, thrown in a mental pit; maybe someone told you to give up on your dream because it will amount to nothing, to that we say, the enemy meant it for evil, but God turns it around for our good.

If you are facing such a situation right now, I am here to tell you that "it's turning around in your favor, and it's working out for your good." Through every trial that we face, we are growing in faith, patience, and love. Our character is being molded, and we are becoming more and more in the image of God. Our purpose is becoming more evident.

God is still the miracle worker. His word is truth, and He is faithful. Is there anything too hard for the Lord?

I will not trade my experiences bringing forth our three beautiful blessings for anything.

1 Robles, Brittany, "Are You Being Induced? Here's What You Need To Know" Postpartum Trainer, MD (Posted March 28, 2021). Retrieved from: https://postpartumtrainer.com/induce-labor/

PROPHETESS RUTH DENTE is a multi-award-winning Gospel Singer/Songwriter, Certified Master Life Coach, Clinical Counsellor, and Ordained minister passionate about God's Kingdom.

Prophetess Ruth is also a member of the History Maker's Transformation Council and founder of Emerge – Mentor

Me Program empowering Women, Youth, and Families to pursue and achieve their Passion and Purpose.

She currently has six solo Music Albums and has won Canada Glass Awards Female vocalist of the year for 2 years consecutively, Artist of the year 2017, and has also been nominated for numerous GMA Covenant Awards, including Gospel Album of the year.

An entrepreneur at heart, she started her own Fashion line, Modisch Couture, in 2016, and on many occasions, she gives back to her community. Prophetess Ruth and her husband have three beautiful girls.

Contact: info@ruthdente.com

https://www.instagram.com/ruthdente/

http://www.facebook.com/ruthdente

http://www.ruthdente.com

17.

LEARNING TO WALK AGAIN

Christie-Ann Nicholas

From the oldest to the youngest amongst us, we all have dreams for the future. Plans that we will hopefully see-through, but sometimes there are major or minor setbacks that delay us from seeing our plans to completion. I was once told that those setbacks are just setups for something greater.

For as long as I can remember, I have always loved the creative things in life. People said that left-handed people tend to be highly creative, and I happened to be one of them. I would write songs, make my own melodies, write poems, and perform them. I loved dramatic arts. I enjoyed doing plays, and as I got older even went to film school. My passion was making films, acting, and directing. Yet, every plan for my life that I have ever had has never gone according to plan, so much so that I asked God what the point was?

My family and friends encouraged me to use my creative talents and do something, but I procrastinated, got scared, and had many doubts. As soon as I believed, I was finally ready to move forward with the pandemic hit, and a lot of opportunities I had were lost. I now had to focus on paying my bills and taking care of my home without a job. By the end of March, I was employed full-time and had a hard time navigating my job, doing what I really wanted to do, and being isolated from my family.

I gave up all things creative and isolated myself falling into a depression. I kept asking God how I could be happy. I knew this is not where I wanted to be, but I could not get out of it. Watching my family and friends start businesses and YouTube channels made me feel like I wasted my time at work. I was not looking at how much work they were putting into these new ventures.

I just saw the result, and I realized I was making excuses for myself. I may not have had the resources, but I could have started somewhere. I remembered a year before I had started making videos on Instagram of things and situations that had made me upset, but after my grandfathers' passing, I stopped. Amid the pandemic and my depression, I started to make them again, but I could not really keep up. My heart was not all there. I was consumed with work and feeling like I did not have enough time in the day to do what I really wanted.

By December, my creative spark had reignited, and I was looking for a way to balance my job and passions. The New Year was quickly approaching, and I had so many ideas; I was looking forward to them coming to fruition, but life had other plans. Then, in the early morning of December 10th, I broke my ankle on my way to work.

This was the worst pain I had ever felt, but I was in shock, and I do not think I really comprehend what was happening. I called my husband, who rushed to my aid and helped me back inside, as I did not fall far from home. I had to make the call to my mom while remaining calm; it did not work. When my husband tried to remove my boot, I cried out in pain, telling him I felt something moving. My mind refused to let me believe that I broke my ankle. The paramedics were called, and they arrived shortly after. They took me into the ambulance, and I was off to the hospital without my husband due to the pandemic.

After many x-rays and keeping my family updated, the doctor came to my room and confirmed what I did not want to hear; I had broken my ankle, but I could not cry; I was shocked. My brother picked me up about an hour later with my foot in a cast, trying to navigate the crutches. I set up a follow-up appointment for the next week. I was out of work indefinitely; due to my work as a security guard, my job was mostly walking and standing, and I could barely do both. My first night was horrible, I was in so much pain, and I could not get comfortable. I was miserable and angry. There were only a couple of weeks left until Christmas!

At my follow-up appointment the next week, I was told there might be a possibility of having surgery. My husband and I discussed staying with my mom, who lived a couple of cities away, to help me with my recovery because I could not do much on my own. I did just that and recovered at my mom's house. On Christmas Eve, I was admitted to the hospital to have surgery. I spent the next few days in a lot of pain, but I celebrated with my husband.

I had started to become withdrawn, upset, and quite emotional. How could this happen to me? Why did God allow this to happen? What did I do wrong? My mom encouraged me to do things that would help better myself, but in all honesty, it went in one ear and out the other because I was not done having a pity party. On January 7th, two days before my 30th birthday, I had my permanent cast on and was told I would have it for 4 weeks. Looking at my scar and how ugly it was made me feel so damaged. I was afraid that I would not even enjoy my birthday, but my family and friends were there for me, loving and supporting me. Finally, on February 4th, my cast came off, and now the real work would begin, learning to walk again.

After my cast came off, it was like I had a weight lifted; I suddenly felt inspired to do the things I wanted to do two years prior. I still had a lot of healing to do physically and emotionally, but I was ready. All the creative ideas started flowing so quickly that I had to write them down on my phone. I talked to my mom, grandma, brothers, aunts, and uncles about my ideas. I was just so excited!

Even though I was injured, God placed before me the opportunity to make good on the plans I had forgotten. It was right in front of me, and I was ready to take it. I had seen enough videos and researched enough to see what needed to be done, but suddenly I was afraid again. Rather than ignoring all the outside noise, I was more concerned with what people would think about my ideas.

Learning to walk did not make it any easier, and before I knew it, I was right back to my pity party. It was frustrating not being able to do the things I once could. Knowing that I was limited made me feel that way internally as well. My injury replayed in my mind like a movie. All the pain I felt, the fear, all of it. I was traumatized and did not want to admit it. I was going through a process that not many around me could understand, and it was very overwhelming.

Going from two crutches and a cast to two crutches and no cast was not exactly easy. I could not trust my foot. The doctor told me I could put pressure on it and walk, but it was so painful. I ended up only using my good leg and crutches for another week before I really started trying to walk. I could not wear shoes; my foot was always swollen and extremely discolored. I felt like I was a burden to my mom, and we both knew it was not my fault, but that did not stop me from feeling useless. All the things I used to do by myself, all the things I had enjoyed doing before my injury, I could no longer do, which left me devastated. I did not realize just how much work it would take into my recovery and how long it would be before I could walk strong and tall on my own two feet.

Eventually, I recovered enough and was able to do many things by myself, but I had a strong fear of outside. As I grew stronger and could walk without using one of my crutches, I was afraid that I would fall again, even if the ground were dry. I could barely walk on the grass without stumbling, let alone go up and down the stairs. My nephew and niece often came over, and I would get so frustrated because I could not play with them and be the aunty I used to be for them. My nephew used to call me "crutch lady," which made me laugh because he processed it at seven years old. He now calls me "healing foot lady" as I no longer use crutches.

When everyone else would be asleep, I would be wide awake because I could not stop thinking about my life and what led up to this very moment. I lived in my mother's house, recovering from a broken ankle with an ugly scar and metal in my foot. The only way to forget was to watch movies. I streamed many movies during my recovery, and it would always bring me back to the same place. It was time to do something that I loved for a change.

I was in a constant battle with myself. I wanted to change my life, I wanted to pursue my passion, but I would sit in bed, unmotivated, and still using my injury as an excuse for why I could not do what I needed to do from my bed. Finally, my mom was there again to encourage me, and she talked me into joining an event called *"Be Confident Challenge" with Dr. Keith Johnson.* For the first time in a long while, I finally started to understand some of the problems in my life. To own up to my mistakes and understand where confidence really comes from. It taught me that I needed to invest in myself.

I started writing my goals and plans in a journal as well as on my phone. A lot of the ideas started coming to me at night when it was quiet. I did not want it to just come to a screeching halt again, so I was pacing myself this time. I started to build my ideas and expand on them; I would then talk it over with my mom and husband.

During this time, my mom was in the process of writing her anthology and doing some blogging. One of my aunt's had so graciously volunteered me to write them for my mom. I was confident with writing as it comes naturally to me, but still, I was hesitant, taking everything slowly. When I was finished, however, I felt good about what I had written. I had a conversation with my nephew, and it inspired me to write a children's book. A friend of mine made a post about children's shows, which inspired me to create a children's television show. The inspiration was coming from everywhere.

Suddenly I had more ideas than I originally thought, and the videos I made in previous years came to mind as a podcast. I spoke to my best friend about it, and he immediately started writing up my podcast plan. Within two hours, I created my plan, my topics, and the duration of my show. All I needed to do was take pictures and come up with an intro and outro.

All the plans I had previously imagined for myself were taking a different direction, and I was okay with that. I was starting to find my way again, and this time I would not let my injury stop me. Although I was limited in some aspects, I decided I would persevere. As the province entered its third lockdown, the idea for a parody came to me. I could not go to sleep. I was so excited. I wrote the song and recorded it in one day. I made a video the very next day. I was so proud of the work that I had done and realized that I could get it done if I really put my mind to it.

Living in my mother's house gave me both the opportunity and tools I needed to do so. I remembered my passion for writing, for creating, for filming. I wanted to see all my ideas come to life. It takes a lot of work, but I was finally ready to take it seriously. The only issue was where to start. Because of my family and friends, I finally figured out where to begin.

My injury made me feel depressed, lost, and like a burden. I questioned God so many times because I could not accept my situation. I believed that I was satisfied with working full time and then pursuing my passions on the side. God showed me that everything happens for a reason. I may not have understood the reason at that time, as I watched others progress in life while I felt stagnant. I was not living someone else's life; mine is a story that no one else could tell. My injury reignited the spark for what I genuinely loved to do. It allowed me to assess my life and change course, and change it again because I didn't particularly appreciate where I was headed.

At 30 years old and recovering from a broken ankle, I thought that it was too late to do what I really wanted, but the pandemic has taught me that anyone can start over, change the direction they want to go in life, and do whatever it is that truly makes them happy. Of course, I still have much work to do when it comes to my ankle, but at least now, I will not be sitting down in sorrow or unmotivated because I have found my purpose. And when I finally have the house I desire, I will be sure to have a creative space for all my ideas and myself.

In life, we face numerous challenges, some that will propel you and many that will try to hold you back, but you can always change the direction of your life by changing your outlook. It might be terrible for a time but ask yourself what you can learn from your situation, even if it was at no fault of your own. Do not restrict your emotions. Go ahead, and embrace them. Then, use those same emotions to fuel you, propel you forward into your purpose, into your destiny, whatever that may look like, take the step.

Christie-Ann is a singer, writer, and actress. At the young age of seven, Christie-Ann developed a passion for creative arts. Inspiring her to become a vocalist, featured on several albums, and was
involved in various productions. In addition, Christie-Ann wrote many poems and short stories.

Christie-Ann enrolled in Toronto Film School, graduating with honors, where she wrote and directed a short film dedicated to her sister and went on to host a television show, "Open Mic."
Christie-Ann is currently working on her first podcast series and hopes to create books and television shows for families and direct short films.

cgnoreiga@gmail.com

Instagram: @chrissiegrace_

Facebook: Christie-Ann Nicholas

18.

BEHIND CLOSED DOORS

Vanya Caprietta

Pur·pose
/ˈpərpəs/ *noun*; The reason for which something is done or created or for which something exists.

In life, hundreds of people, especially women, get caught up with this infamous question: What is my purpose? Let me tell you; that four-word sentence haunted me for years until one day I had the guts, or should I say the Faith, to have the 'Purpose' conversation with God!

You see, I have a Type-A Personality; where are all my Type-A Personality people at? I see you in the back trying to hide. But, it's ok to admit your traits because it helps you understand your strengths and weaknesses. So, for those who are still trying to figure out if you are a Type-A person, here are some traits.

- You have a lot of ambition
- You need to complete set goals promptly
- You are task-focused
- You are competitive
- You are most likely to experience stress when faced with delays that affect your success

That, my friend, is a Type-A personality in a nutshell. So, with that being said, what are you? Assess yourself; I had to do it too. I, Vanya Caprietta, confess that I was highly driven by competition and extremely goal-oriented, especially in my career, motherhood, and marriage. I was so driven to be recognized as accomplished that I overlooked my purpose and I, unfortunately, became desensitized to God. I was swamped trying to obtain a goal that I missed, or should I say that I tuned out God's voice.

How did I know that I had missed his voice? I know, that you may be asking yourself if you too have missed God's voice. I knew I had missed God's voice the moment that I found myself lying in bed in the middle of the night, with tears streaming down my eyes. The moment I couldn't sleep because I was battling with thoughts of quitting my monotonous retail job. The moment when I began to question God about my unaccomplished situation, simply out of fear and insecurity. That night was the beginning of my journey of being *pursued by purpose*.

For the nine years leading up to this Purpose moment, I was so *goal-focused* and *not God-focused.* In 2009, I graduated with Honors from York University, with a Bachelor of Arts and B Bachelor of Education. Immediately after graduation, I got married to my amazing hubby, Pearry Caprietta. After we came back from our honeymoon, I hit the ground, actively applying in-person to schools and the school board in my region. I was determined to achieve my goal of having a dream job. I had my entire life planned out and was eager to enter the Education field as a teacher.

My goal was to become an interactive Female Black teacher who was passionate about representing the voices of minorities in the classroom. Shockingly, an unpleasant surprise met me at the Board, which had placed a hiring freeze in my area. In plain terms, they were not hiring any more staff for the year and would maintain the roster they previously had. I couldn't understand how that was even possible. This devastation triggered my Type A Personality…your girl was stressed, overwhelmed, and felt defeated. I had planned to be a teacher all my life, and I knew that this career was my purpose. Or was it?

Let's fast forward to 2018, the year that God destroyed strongholds and curses in my life. After nine years of periodically applying to different boards and private schools, I gave up in frustration. Finally, I settled for working retail, but God's favor was on my life, even in this field. God's favor is so amazing! Although not in my teaching position, I was allowed to be an Assistant Operations Manager for a retail branch. Let's be honest, it was a good job, but there was still something missing. I was missing that fulfillment and joy. I was still missing my purpose!

Every year in December, I seek God for a scripture that would give me direction for the year. That year he gave me the scripture Joshua 1:9.
Joshua 1:9 *"Have I not commanded you? Be strong and courageous. Do not be afraid; do not be discouraged, for the LORD your God will be with you wherever you go."*

Listen, after pushing what seemed like a dead dream for nine years, you need a word like that from the Lord. I remember, one day, I went over to see my Grama with the kids. Shout out to my two-time Cancer survivor Grama! In a casual conversation, my very Jamaican grama said, "Why you don't try to get a teaching job from the board?" I just stared at her with a deep feeling of shame.

I didn't want to try again. I didn't want to resurrect a dream that was dead for the past nine years. I think deep down inside, I didn't have faith because of the fear of rejection. It is crazy that a small, four-letter word (Fear) can paralyze you from believing and trusting God again. Oh my! That will preach! I don't know if you have buried your dream, but the same God that rose from the dead can resurrect your dream. My grama's voice woke me up out of sorrow. She then said softly, "Just try again and see." I assured her that I would try again. When I got home, I got on my computer and tried again! I applied to the school board and left it at that.

I did not hear back from the school board for about two months. Then, finally, one day, I sat at my computer in a daze. For some reason, that day, I reacted differently to rejection. My reaction surprised me. Instead of just slumping into a state of depression, I got angry. I wasn't angry at the Lord, but I was angry with the devil. I had enough! I got up from my desk, went into my closet, and began to pray. This was a different prayer. It was not a "woe is me" type of prayer, but a "devil get your hands off my destiny and career" prayer. The scripture Joshua 1:9 was on a sticky note in my prayer closet. A sudden rush to cry out to the Lord poured over me.

I was like the children of Israel, calling out to be saved from bondage. My God heard me! He SPOKE! Yes, God SPEAKS! He can speak to you through his word (the

Bible), or he could use a person or speak audibly. I had finally gotten quiet enough to hear his voice; the days of missing him were over! ***He told me to fast for fourteen days and pray with my husband in the morning and night.*** Yeah, you already know I had a moment! I had to ask, 'God, is that you? Are really speaking?" I am a wife and a working mother with four beautiful children to give you context. I had no idea how I would find the time to accomplish this task that God had set before me. However, as I began to reason my way out of this 'Purpose Assignment,' I remembered that scripture again. "Be strong and courageous. Do not be afraid; do not be discouraged, for the LORD your God will be with you wherever you go."

In February of 2018, I began to seek the face of the Lord with my husband. I only had one expectation, and that was to encounter God every time I entered my Prayer Closet. Every time I went into my closet to pray, it was different; my experience was never the same. There were moments of repentance and deliverance, moments of vulnerability and healing. In my Prayer Closet, nothing was hidden from my Heavenly Father. He spoke to me concerning childhood traumas, selfish and prideful ambitions, and unforgiveness. Y'all, it was as though I was entering an Emergency Operating room twice a day; however, I was not forced but had a desire to be made whole. I do not know about you, but when you begin to see change happening, there is a thirst for more. I wanted to keep drinking from the river of living water because I saw growth towards wholeness that I had never seen before. God had a plan to bring wholeness to my life so that I could walk in my purpose authentically.

During this time, God would send confirmation after

confirmation from my mother, father, sisters, and my sisters-in-love. One day, my mother called to check on my children and I, but that conversation flowed into words of encouragement to keep pushing forward to accomplishing my dreams. Most of my family didn't know that I was fasting and praying about a release for my purpose. Still, coincidentally they would give me words of wisdom and encouragement concerning my career and family. My sisters-in-love were even led to gather with me and pray. We experienced a breakthrough that night. God was sending signs of hope to keep meeting him every day for that two-week period. We could even say that Purpose began to pursue me.

On the last day of my prayer time with my husband, we met in the living room and began to worship. We were singing, and the spirit of the Lord took over. I knew that the Lord had taken over our voices because my husband began to sing new melodies from heaven prophetically. It was as though I was being engulfed with the presence of the Lord, and I could not contain my tears of joy. My husband then shifted into prophetic prayer and began to declare blessings and release over my life.

As he was praying, I heard a loud voice say, "You will never amount to anything!" I looked at my husband and asked him if he heard that. He confirmed that he did not hear anything. I told him that I heard a loud voice saying, "You will never amount to anything." He said, "Vanya, someone has cursed your career." I was flabbergasted.

People do not realize the power of their words. While growing up, I have heard the saying, "sticks and stones will break your bones, but your words will never hurt you." Correction! Sticks and stones hurt, and so do words. People can consciously and unconsciously curse your destiny through their words. The bible says" that death and life are in the power of the tongue, and those who love it will eat its fruit." – *Proverbs 18:21.*

This did not scare Pearry; this gave him direction on how to pray. We stood together holding hands and began to break that curse through prayer. People, this was the mega deliverance that God had planned for me. This was beyond my expectation! After we prayed, I felt a sense of peace. God did a miraculous thing that night, my faith crushed my fears, and I began to believe again. I had finally stopped tuning out the voice of God; instead, I became attuned to his voice!

The following morning, I got up with JOY! The joy of the Lord was my strength. I was in awe that I had done a fourteen-day prayer challenge and had a supernatural encounter with the Lord. I felt unstoppable! I did my regular morning routine and checked my email before heading out to work. As I opened my email, I froze in shock, and there was a letter from the School Board. It stated that I should attend a sign-up session and bring my documents to be placed on the Emergency Supply list. This was the miracle job offer email that I had been waiting on for nine years! I permit you to **SHOUT** now! I know I did! I called Pearry into the room and told him that God had given me a job without an interview. That's the God I serve!

This Chapter, or let's call it a Testimony, is not about just acquiring a job; it's about pushing past insurmountable situations and understanding the power of prayer. When God instructed me to pray for two weeks in my closet, this was the birth of a greater plan that he had for me. This "Prayer Closet" experience revealed that I had authority, which gave me boldness in my prayer life. This experience springboarded me into a life of intercession and cultivated a passion for teaching women about the power of prayer. I began to realize that becoming a teacher was not my end goal. God did not design me just for the classroom, but he is using my gift of teaching to push me into a bigger purpose.

This chapter started with the definition of Purpose. They characterize purpose as a ***noun,*** which is considered a person, place, or thing. However, I now have a new perspective on the word Purpose because it should not be based on a position or destination, but it should be seen as a cultivated journey. *In this season, I pray that you will have a "prayer closet" experience that helps unravel your purpose. I pray that you begin to speak bold declarations and prayers over your life. You will not be limited by your past experiences but will be propelled into greatness. It's time to begin to walk by faith into your purpose in Jesus' Name.*

I want to leave you with this quote from one of my mentors, Rev. Nicole Salmon, **"Purpose is not a place you get to, it's a place you live from."**

Vanya Caprietta is a Wife, Mother of four, dynamic Educator, and passionate Prayer Coach. She is the visionary behind "The Prayer Closet," an online community platform that strives to empower women to develop and maintain a strong prayer altar with God. Her mission is to teach women how to utilize their weapon of prayer effectively. Once you begin to use your weapon of prayer, things will shift, change lives, and it will transform your minds.

Vanya's other passion is her new clothing company called 'Līf (life) Apparel Co, a Christian Apparel company that creates BOLD Christian wear that speaks Life! In addition, she loves cooking, singing with her husband, and just cuddling with her kids in her spare time.

Contact: vcaprietta@gmail.com

Instagram: @vee_alexei

Facebook: Vee Vee

19.

LIFE'S LESSONS

Debra Wright

When you walk through some tough times, you begin to wonder about the purpose of all the pain. I know that many of us can identify with this because we have all been there at some point in our lives.

I thought about this for so long and wondered so many times why God allowed me to go through the fire time and time again. As a teenager growing up in a strict Christian home, sometimes I felt like I was missing out on life because I could not do quite a few things that other young people my age could do. This was a big issue because I wanted to go out with my friends to places they would go and stay out later than seven pm. Yes, I know that seems like nothing looking back now, but for an eighteen-year-old, it feels like your whole world is going to fall apart.

In retrospect, this was not so bad, the protectiveness of my parents. They just really loved me and wanted what was best for me. 'However,' In the middle of my eighteenth year, I decided to take a chance, and in the end, I ended up in pain. I grew up in a small village in the Caribbean. My girlfriends and I would fantasize about meeting our prince charming. The man we would meet, fall in love with, get married, and live happily ever after. One day in late September of 1985, I was out with my mom, and I met a young man. After getting to know one another for a short time, I fell madly in love with him and had the time of my life. After that, I could only focus on my relationship and nothing else.

Being in love made me ignore all the warning bells that were going off. I wanted to be in his company constantly, even against my parents' wishes. Unlike North America, an eighteen-year-old is not considered an *adult* in the Caribbean. Parents are still in control, and there is no government assistance if you decide to leave home.

During this relationship, I endured some real pain and heartache, but I was in love. I was willing to go the distance because I thought this was the love that I wanted. When the relationship eventually came to an end, I never closed the door.

The person that comes into your life is not necessarily bad, but it may be that they are not good for you at that time or not at all. I enjoyed a lot of good times, but it also came with heartaches along the way. My trust was broken because of lies, and in the end, I had to leave home to make a new life for myself in a different country. While I carried the pain from the breakup in my heart, I still yearned for this man, but I had to keep it moving. Unfortunately, there was no closure because we just stopped communicating.

Key Fact: *When you are in a relationship that ends, make sure to close all doors because they have a way of coming back to haunt you.*

Forcefully letting go of this relationship was painful

for me because, honestly, I had loved him with all my heart. School and my new environment became the focus. I started gaining independence and slowly moved on with my life. Life was good as I was no longer living under my parent's roof. I started to fly somewhat solo, learning how to navigate my surroundings in a new place. It is kind of what we are going through now with this Covid-19 pandemic; we must learn to navigate all the changes in our lives. We are living with new realities. We must stay inside and socially distant from family and friends. I understand this very well; I was away from my parents and siblings and had to learn to navigate without them; just as this virus, we will come out stronger.

I was about to graduate from college in the fall of eighty-seven when an old friend from back home came to visit. We started communicating, and we became better friends. We eventually realized we had feelings for each other, and after six months of dating, we got married. We were together for 25 years and raised a family. After that, however, life began to change, and I could not really understand what was happening to us. My idea of family was based on what I saw as a child and as a young woman.

My life was great while I was growing up. Besides getting into trouble and wanting to have more freedom as a young person, life was indeed fine. I watched my parents navigate life's ups and downs with prayer, love, and understanding.

These examples of family life should be what I based my hopes and dreams on for our own family. Unfortunately, the relationships I found myself in did not match up with my expectations. I had children, and I tried to align my family that way. It worked for a while, but when a couple is no longer working together in harmony as a family, there is bound to be major problems. The bible says: "Two cannot walk together unless they agree." Some basic things caused challenges that I had to work through. No matter what I tried, we could not make it come together. Whether it was the finances, the kids, and eventually religion, nothing worked.

As a mother, you always put your children first. I remember a time when my children were relatively young and became sick at the same time. I did not have my driver's license, and I could not find anyone to drive me to the hospital. There and then, I vowed never to let that happen to me again, and this drove me to get my driver's license finally. *Situations force you to evaluate where you are and take necessary actions.*

Even though my children were thriving, I felt like I was dying inside. I had a marriage that drained me of my essence. There was a lot of criticism, but there was no communication. My life as it was made me feel less than a woman. A woman likes to be complimented and made to feel she is beautiful. However, when her spouse does not communicate, she somewhat begins to lose her self-esteem and self-confidence. That was me; I became withdrawn and sometimes unsure how to keep it moving. One thing that kept me going was the beautiful thought that my children would grow up, and I would be able to do the things I wanted to do with my life.

Key: *Communication is key in a relationship*

In any relationship, communication is key. Between a

husband and his wife, communication is important to keep the marriage going. Likewise, at work, with siblings, parents, children, and friends, we all need to communicate to move our relationships forward. It does not matter the nature of our relationship; we need to have good communication. I tried everything that I could to change the communication in my family. I suggested counseling, overnight trips to see what would help to make the relationship work—all to no avail.

How can you live in a home and not say a word to each other, or you speak, and no one answers you? This was my situation, and it went on year after year.

One day I laid on my bed, and I just cried out to God; I said, "Lord! I need you right now; please speak to me." I heard an audible voice say to me, read Judges 5:12. It says, *"Wake up, wake up, Deborah! Sing a song!"*
I was floored. The God of heaven called me by name. I fell on my face and cried out to him. You see, during this season, I was drowning in the depths of loneliness, and my blood pressure was through the roof. So, for the Lord to hear and answer gave me such a lift in my spirit.

The situation at home did not change, but there were some good days where we enjoyed ourselves and had a measure of peace. I looked forward to those days. It was as if one was alone in the desert and desperately in need of water.

As the years passed, many rough patches crept up, and I felt that I could not catch a break as much as I tried. In addition, my health was very challenged. On a family vacation to Pennsylvania in July 2001, I felt exhausted and lethargic. I could not understand what was happening to me.

When we arrived at our destination, I got on the phone with one of my cousins, and I happened to look in the mirror; at first, I thought maybe it was just because I was speaking that my mouth seemed twisted. I checked again and realized that there was a definite problem. We had just driven eight hours in the heat, and I was scared. I was taken to the hospital, and because I was hypertensive, the physicians thought maybe I was having a stroke but thanked God it was not that. I was diagnosed with Bell's Palsy.

With the diagnosis, I was able to get some medicine to help the swelling of the nerve go down. My upcoming testimony was what I cherish the most. This happened on the weekend, and we returned home on Monday evening. I was given an appointment to see a specialist the next day, and he gave me six months for it to go away; for *some people, it never does*. I was scared, but that night we had a church service, and I asked for prayer. The man of God prophesied that although the doctors said six months to see healing, I would return and sing for the Lord in six days. I accepted it and went home. On Sunday morning, I was able to sing and testify of the goodness of God. If you see me today, you could never tell that for a short time in my life, my entire face was twisted to the left.

Relationships can be incredibly challenging, and many times we go into it with unrealistic expectations. For me, I had the mindset of happily ever after, but from that fairytale perspective. I was an avid romance novel fan. I devoured them with veracity. The books would take me away from my reality, even just for that time and space. I was hungry to feel loved, and during one of my vacation trips, I was reconnected with my first love. Remember I said previously you need to close doors when you go through a breakup? It is imperative to do so. Some doors that we do not close leave room for some big surprises. This meeting was not premeditated because we had lost contact for about thirteen years. This chance meeting brought to the forefront all the hurt of the past and the present.

I was enduring a relationship where I did not feel worthy and appreciated, I was harboring hurt, and now I was reconnected with someone from my past. How do I now navigate my new reality? My heart was torn, and I was not thinking straight. I decided to keep in contact and throw caution to the wind. As you can probably guess, it was disastrous. I had just made a terrible situation worse, and I personally did not know how to get myself freed from the emotions. I felt loved and cherished; I had someone that I could talk to, and I felt like they connected with me too. Many people talk about soulmates, but do you really understand what it means? The dictionary states: *"a person ideally suited to another as a close friend or romantic partner."* So, when we have soulmates and become intimate, we acquire soul ties.

You may ask, "What are you talking about?"

According to the Urban dictionary, a soul tie is "a spiritual/emotional connection you have to someone after being intimate with them, usually engaging in sexual intercourse. The feeling that you can't be rid of them from your mind and your life, even when you are far away, you still feel as if you are a part of each other as if you've given up some intangible part of yourself that cannot easily possess again."

So here I am, losing myself to this overwhelming feeling, and my relationship is getting more complicated without knowing how to pull it back. Eventually, I was able to end it. However, the guilt and shame I felt from reconnecting with my old flame had me in a dark place. I wanted to be a good partner, but I felt I let myself and my family down.

I began reading Christian romance novels, and I started noticing a theme throughout my reading novels. As I began reading in a book was one scripture that became my mantra. Although I did not think much of the words I was reading at first, I knew the scripture, but at this point, I was reading to take my mind off my current predicament, not really paying attention.

One day I saw the scripture again, Jeremiah 29:11 *"For I know the plans I have for you, declares the LORD. "They are plans for good and not disaster, to give you a future and hope."*
I also began hearing it on the radio and at church. One day while sitting in my family room reading, I said: "Lord, I am listening; I know you are trying to tell me something." I prayed after that, and I felt that something was going to change, not sure what and how but I knew for sure it would.

For most of my life, I believed in romance and happily ever after; as a matter of fact, I still do.
That marriage ended in divorce, and even though it was wrought with pain, I still mourned the loss of what could

have been. The lessons I have learned are that the pain and hurt that I endured brought me to my purpose in life.

Though my trust was broken many times in the two serious relationships I had, it did not keep me down totally; I would not allow it. I made sure to fight my way back to the top. I started a business when someone told me that I would never be good at it. I went back to school and made sure my children were well-grounded and successful in life.

Through the pains I have suffered, I have been able to help other people who are hurting by listening to them, giving them some strategies to help them navigate the obstacles they are facing.

While I was experiencing the pain, I had no idea that God allowed those situations to know the purpose he had for my life. These failed and painful relationships did not cause me to lose faith in humanity; I still believe in happily ever after. I was able to forgive and trust again. I remarried a few years later. One of the main things that got me through my journey was being able to forgive. God gave me the heart to forgive any circumstance. It is not always easy, but it is definitely worth it for my peace of mind.

Debra M. Wright is Forgiveness Life Coach, Motivational Speaker, and a Bestselling Author.

Debra is an affiliate with Americas' #1 Confidence Coach Dr. Keith Johnson and the Destiny Coaching group.

As a forgiveness life coach, she has had many situations in her life that have set her on this journey. Her passion is to help women that have gone through broken relationships, by separation or divorce, to get to a place of freedom from resentment, anger, and bitterness. Debra will take you on the forgiveness journey and help you to let go so you can live a better life.

Debra is the host of her show Real Talk Forgiveness on the Speakup and Empower Network and Host of Kingdom

Authors Forum on the Virtuous Entertainment TV Network (VETVN)

She is an award-winning Leadership and Speaker with Christopher Leadership Lumen Association.

Contact: debra@debramwright.com

https://www.instagram.com/debramwright1/

https://www.facebook.com/Debrawright21/

https://www.debramwright.com/

I

A QUEEN

The trouble
The pain
The heartache
The shame
For his worth
and not for your gain
   The disillusionment The yearning
The babies….. yet
Still without learning.
Is he worth it?
Is he worth your passion,
your pride?
Although he's taking you
on a love ride
Keep your head
and stand no pain
You've got nothing to lose
and more to gain
   For without him, you'll be happy and without pain
And a queen you'll be
In your home to reign

   Written by: Cherie

11

I Feel Your Pain!!

I feel your pain; I see your struggles

   I was exactly where you are

   Call on me if you ever need me
   I will be there in a hurry

   I've walked your struggles; I've nursed your pain
   The journey was not all in vain

   Every crystal raindrop of tears created a beautiful
   rainbow for someone somewhere

   I've grown from your struggles
   I've learned from your pain.

   It may seem hard, but know that you can do the same.

   Soon you'll become aware
   There's light in the darkness of all the struggles
   through the storms and the rain

   Yes! I feel your struggles
   I see your pain

I've walked in those shoes just the same

I've nursed your pain
I felt lost and ashamed

But now I've grown
I am aware that there's a true purpose to all our struggles and our pain

Love and light to all and everyone who is struggling with pain

Written by Rose Marie Young.

CONCLUSION

Well, you have come to the end of this book, and I am sure you sat there reading and wondering how did they all make it to this point in their lives.

In the beginning, we met Carla and her journey looking through the rearview mirror and how she found herself and went towards her dreams. It took courage under tremendous pressure.

Christie-Ann faced her parents' divorce with pain and trepidation, realizing that her worst fears were manifesting. She had to find the power within herself to make her marriage work and not follow in her parents' footsteps. Her journey continued as she had to relearn how to walk after breaking her ankle and seeing her future change dramatically for the better.

Oh, how can we forget Dr. Maria? After fifty-three years, she lost the love of her life and found the courage to live and start that new chapter in life, still honoring the man she loved and doing great things to help families realize that they matter.

I am really blessed by Pauline's story of how the words people speak over your life can affect you if you allow it to. Pauline realized that what her guidance counselor told her was false, and she is now moving on to bigger and better things in life. Never listen to the lies of the enemy; he comes to steal, kill and destroy. Believe in yourself.

What about Cindy? She came to Canada an innocent young woman; she struggled to keep her head above water while navigating the ins and outs of the immigration maze. Yet, she was triumphant and now has owned not one but two homes all by herself. Maybe you might be that person reading her story, and this gives you faith to continue, never giving up until you achieve what you set out to do.

Rose, a vibrant young woman experienced not one but two traumatic vehicular accidents that changed the trajectory of her life set her on a downward spiral of pain and depression; however, she rose and has found her life's passion and purpose. She now coaches people dealing with traumatic injuries and situations.

Rev. Marlene's life is a testimony; her mother had two options, bear the shame of being pregnant by a much older man or abort her unborn child, but she held on and kept her beautiful daughter, who is a blessing to everyone that knows her.

Apostle Glen left his homeland without a real plan to live in the United States of America. He said goodbye to friends and family and made his way across the seas. The border patrol knew that he was not planning on leaving the USA, but we know that God ordered his steps even when he had not totally surrendered his life to him. Now he is walking in his purpose and serving God.

Having faith the size of a mustard seed is how Anna describes her journey. Anna wanted so badly to be a mother, and when that vision for her life did not materialize, she found other ways to fill the void in her heart. Finally, she found her purpose and is living life on her terms. This, too, shall pass.

Lovemore, yes, we need to love more deeply. This beautiful soul has had many challenges to overcome, and I can attest to the metamorphosis seen in her today. She lights up a room with her smile and personality, bringing joy to those around her. So, fly Butterfly, you have been through the cocoon, and the waters all squeezed out of you to introduce us to this beautiful butterfly.

Aww, Nicole is one of the iron sharpeners; she speaks with you in love but with such authority. Her struggles have made her the advocate that she is today for Mental Health. Her dedication and compassion will go a long way.

Rev. Blessing knew that God had told her and the family to get up and leave the land of Nigeria and migrate to Canada. Through all that this family endured, we know that God was on their side. Her life is a miracle and a testimony to the readers.

As a four-year-old child, Cheryl had already stated that she was a big girl now. Having witnessed her mother's death, she knew that she had to do things for herself even at a tender age. Her struggles equipped her to be the independent woman she is today. A loving soul is always willing to help someone in pain.

Carlton watched his life changed as a young boy by illness. So many childhood illnesses cause children to be withdrawn and sometimes very sad and emotional. Being diagnosed with a life-altering disease had that effect on him. However, he would lead a normal life with the help of God, modern medicine, family, and music. Ensure that if you know of a child with a life-changing illness, please do all you can to help them feel that they matter.

I loved Prophetess Ruth's story. We know that many women love to recount and share their birthing stories with other young women, and sometimes it scares them when it is their turn to give birth. Sometimes when these conversations come up, you can move away from it if it affects you or ask them to stop. Everyone's experience is different. Ruth's experience was a miracle, and yours can be as well.

Meeting Vanya was fascinating. She is a unique and beautiful individual who is so full of life. In addition, she is a prayer warrior. Her journey as a teacher did not go as planned, but when she went before God, he heard her prayer and answered it for her and her family.

Oh, what do you know? It is my turn! Putting this book together was very interesting, overwhelming, and at the same time, required the labor of love. My stories were born out of the experiences that occurred in my personal life. I defied the doctors and had three babies after experiencing two miscarriages in wanting to have a child so badly. I felt as if something was tugging at my heartstrings, and it did not matter how much I had suffered; I wanted my babies. My life's lessons taught me how to forgive and move on in life, thus enabling me to now share Forgiveness with others, teaching them the principles of forgiving themselves and others.

Let us always remember that the trials come to make us stronger. For example, if you look at trees in a storm, the wind blows them hard, but we cannot see that it is causing the roots to sink deeper into the ground. Stand firm! You are Victorious!

I trust that this book has allowed you to re-evaluate your life and recognize that not everything bad happens to harm you; it could be one or more situations that lead you to your purpose for such a time as this.

Debra M. Wright

Notes

1 Robles, Brittany, "Are You Being Induced? Here's What You Need To Know" Postpartum Trainer, MD (Posted March 28, 2021). Retrieved from: https://postpartumtrainer.com/induce-labor/

Bible Translations used:

New King James, Amplified, NIV, and King James

1 Office of the United Nations High Commissioner for Refugees – Facts. NobelPrize.org. Nobel Media AB 2020. Sat. 21 Nov 2020. <https://www.nobelprize.org/prizes/peace/1981/refugees/facts/>

Publishers Note

Uplifting Stories Of Courage Under Pressure

Thank you again to you, our dear readers; if these stories touched your soul, please feel free to message any co-authors in this book. We have put their social media handles and emails for you to contact us.

If you would like to publish a book with RMK, please email me at:
rmkpublishing2@gmail.com

Other Books by Author

Becoming   Debra   Wright

   Available on Amazon